The
Seashore

The Seashore
and its wildlife

Robert Burton

G. P. Putnam's Sons New York

© Orbis Publishing Limited, London
and Istituto Geografico
de Agostini S.p.A., Novara 1977
SBN: 399-11886-1
Library of Congress Catalog
Card Number: 76-28656
Printed in Italy by IGDA, Novara
Frontispiece: Cape Horn, South America
Right: Shelduck (Tadorna tadorna)

Contents

Introduction

In 1850 severe winter gales cut open a sand dune at Skara Brae on one of the Orkney islands lying north of the Scottish mainland. The sand was blasted away revealing the remains of a Stone Age settlement which in due course was excavated by archaeologists. They found a group of stone huts, complete with stone furnishings and tools, from which they could build up a picture of how the inhabitants had lived. To uncover the huts, the archaeologists had to dig through a midden, an ancient refuse tip which had accumulated around the walls of the huts and spilled over their roofs.

The midden contained the remains of meals eaten thousands of years ago and, among the bones of sheep and cattle, there were countless shells of limpets, cockles and mussels. Without doubt, the Stone Age inhabitants of Skara Brae had used the nearby seashore as a very important source of food. More storms later uncovered another Stone Age settlement, this time at Jarlshof on the neighbouring Shetland Islands. Once again excavations uncovered a midden stuffed with the remains of shellfish dinners, and since then similar middens have been found in many other excavations around the world.

Prehistoric man had obviously looked on the seashore as a good place for filling his belly. Close-packed beds of limpets, periwinkles and mussels provided abundant food even during the winter when his meagre stocks of grain and small herds of animals were dwindling. The habit of shore-collecting must actually have started early in the history of man, long before Skara Brae or Jarlshof were inhabited, and there has even been a suggestion that a life of paddling and swimming in the shallow waters of sea and lake may have been crucial to human evolution. True or not, no one

Left : Pinnacles of hard rock stand out from a beach of volcanic ash on an Icelandic shore

7

Left: A favourite food for thousands of years: mussels are harvested from wooden piles

can doubt that our earliest ancestors must have come down to the seashore in their search for food, as, indeed, do some oriental monkeys nowadays. These eating habits have continued through the ages and even today the shores are visited by collectors of cockles, oysters, periwinkles and shrimps, as well as the plants of the seashore. In Scotland, for instance, four kinds of seaweed were eaten regularly, either raw, fried with oatmeal or made into soup.

In most instances, harvesting the seashore has not progressed beyond the primitive gathering techniques of the Stone Age. The only advance has been to set harvesting quotas or size limits to protect the stocks from overcollecting. Farming the seashore has been limited to the culture of oysters and, more recently, mussels. Oyster farming was developed independently by the Romans and Japanese and is now practised in many parts of the world.

With increased civilization and leisure time, people have also visited the shore and examined its inhabitants for their own sake. The Ancient Greeks, with Aristotle to the fore, examined the natural history of the shore creatures and the

Romans collected decorative seashells, but then the seashore was deserted by the curious until the renaissance of natural history as a pastime in Victorian times. The Industrial Revolution in Britain had produced a middle class with the time and money for leisure pursuits and so people descended on the seashores in masses. Unfortunately, as in all spheres of Victorian natural history, the emphasis was on collecting and the energy that built an empire also led to the pillaging of many beautiful coastal stretches. Nevertheless the foundations of seashore science and, indeed, of marine science as a whole, were laid by the systematic description and cataloguing of specimens collected in these nineteenth-century forays.

The study of seashore life has changed considerably since the Victorians did their collecting and cataloguing. Professional biologists scrutinize the habits of plants and animals more minutely to see how they fit into the general scheme of the shore environment. They use sophisticated techniques and apparatus to study the minutiae of life processes and the results are published in detail and in jargon that is intelligible only to

other biologists. Removing seashore study to higher intellectual planes can take the fun out of the business but this need not be the case. The findings of the scientists can be translated back into everyday language to provide an even greater interest for the enthusiastic shore visitor.

The aim of the following pages is to explain the structure of seashores and describe the communities of plants and animals living on different kinds of shore. Some of the more interesting and typical species are also examined in detail, although there is no catalogue of plant and animal types. Armed with this information, the amateur naturalist can then go and look at the shore in a different light. He will see why some animals live on some shores but not on others and that, for instance, a limpet is not so dull as might seem from a specimen clamped immovably to a rock. He will know that it moves about in search of food and unerringly returns to the same spot.

The immense variety and vast number of different seashore organisms make the list of included species necessarily selective. Naturally, there is emphasis on the more striking and familiar kinds, such as crabs, periwinkles, limpets and

shellfish, but it must not be forgotten that there are many lesser animals. Although easily overlooked they may be more abundant than the familiar animals and have an interest of their own. The sponges for instance are easily passed by, but the reader will see that they are fascinating animals whose lives prove to be most instructive.

It seems hardly necessary to describe what we mean by a seashore, yet as sometimes happens, it is not easy to define an everyday term. The shore is the line of contact between the sea surface and the land. Because of fluctuating water level caused by the tides, the shore forms a strip of ground that is neither wholly marine nor wholly terrestrial in character. We can say simply that the shore lies between high and low tide marks, bounded by land on one side and sea on the other, and that its inhabitants have to be capable of living both in and out of water. Above these amphibious animals live land animals and plants, incapable of surviving immersion, and below live marine species that cannot survive drying up. Yet Nature ignores hard and fast boundaries. At the top of the shore lies the splash zone which is wetted with spray from breaking waves. Land and

Above : An oil spill is the most obvious product of modern technology to hazard the world's shores. Other forms of damage may pass unheeded yet be even more destructive

shore forms of life mingle here. And at the bottom of the shore the very lowest tides sometimes uncover scallops, oysters and other animals which cannot properly be called shore animals. So there is room for argument about what should be included in a comprehensive list of seashore fauna and flora.

Within the past twenty or thirty years the scientific study of seashores has become increasingly important, because the shores are among the many places feeling the pressure of expanding technology and a rising human population. The threats to the safety of seashore life are many. There are problems of overzealous collecting, such as of abalones for their meat and shells, the introduction of alien species that compete with the native species, for instance the slipper limpet (*Crepidula fornicata*) and the giant Japweed (*Sargassum muticum*), first seen in

Above left: The tidal range of a single shore. At low tide a wide beach is exposed to the tropical heat; at high tide waves break against the cliffs
Left: 'Japweed' an alien species of seaweed smothers the native European species

British waters in 1973, and the effects of pollution. Oilslicks from tankers or coastal oilrigs are now an ever-present threat to shorelines. Yet more damaging than any of these is the wholesale destruction or removal of the coastal habitat by industrial development.

The damming of the Ijsselmeer and the reclamation of polders has given the crowded Dutch nation more living room, but at the expense of losing large areas of marine habitat. A similar project has been suggested for the Wash, on the East Anglian coast of England. On the West Coast of Scotland, sheltered sea lochs are polluted by the effluents from alginate and wood pulp factories. Similar stories can be told around the world. Damming of rivers prevents sediments from entering the sea, so beaches disappear. On the other hand, increased soil erosion through clearing tropical forests brings down more sedi-

ments in rivers, so coral reefs are killed off. Hot water from power stations, and sewage are other increasingly common killers.

The damage to seashores everywhere is alarming and it is hardly reassuring to learn of mass destruction in such far-off, secluded places as the Virgin Islands and Tierra del Fuego. There is no possibility of preventing these various acts of vandalism although conservation can be attempted, as happens in other habitats, by the provision of parks or reserves. The formation of marine parks has only begun in the past few years and there are still very few considering the enormous length of the world's coastlines. However, an impressive example has been set by the government of the Cook Islands which has dedicated an entire coral atoll, Manaue Island, as a World Marine Park. It can only be hoped that the example set by these islanders is followed.

Above : The Dutch have reclaimed large areas of land from the sea by building dykes and pumping out the sea. Fertile seabeds are replaced by fertile land

The Formation of the Shore

The varied features of coastlines with their cliffs and bays, beaches and estuaries, are the result of physical forces that have been working at the land's edge for thousands of years. In northern Europe and North America, new coastlines emerged when the land was relieved of the weight of the Ice Age glaciers. Ever since, rain, tides and waves have combined to wear away or build up the original form of the land. In many parts of Europe, Medieval ports, stranded inland or sunk beneath the waves, remind us of the ancient and continuous action of the elements.

The Shape of the Shore

The story of any section of coastline stretches back millions of years to the time when the coastal rocks were first laid down. Rocks inland were eroded by sun and rain, and particles from them were carried down by wind and water to be laid as sand or mud in lakes and seas. As these deposits grew deeper, pressure built up on the lower layers, compressing them and so transforming them into hard rocks.

Sediments were not only formed by rock particles. Chalks and limestones are made up of countless skeletons of microscopic animals that lived near the sea surface and sank to the bottom when dead. Sometimes their bodies did not completely decay and the organic remains were eventually transformed into deposits of oil which were trapped under later sediments. In a similar way, partly decomposed plant remains, in the form of peat, have been changed by pressure into rock-like coal seams. These fossil fuels are usually buried deep under succeeding layers of sediment, and because of this gradual deposition of sediments, one on top of the other, deeper rocks are, of course, older than those nearer the surface.

The sedimentary rocks formed by this primeval moulding process were, in their turn, eroded, often by the action of waves plucking at sea cliffs, to form beaches of sand or pebbles. These became consolidated into sandstone and pudding-stones (conglomerates). Sandstones, formed, of course, from sand, are soft rocks that wear into fine particles; conglomerates, formed from pebbles, look like rough concrete. The difference between land-formed and sea-formed sandstones is that sea sand has been rolled about in the waves and the grains are rounded rather than angular.

These rocks were laid down in horizontal layers and such strata are often distinctive features of our coastal cliffs. However, cliffs often reveal strata thrown at careless angles, sometimes vertical and occasionally tipped right over. These bizarre patterns were caused by the huge upheavals that crumpled the Earth's crust and threw up the mountain ranges. The crust became corrugated by these gigantic earth movements, and sometimes a complete corrugation can be seen where two oppositely tilted strata meet to form an arch or basin.

The pressures of mountain building sometimes broke the strata as cleanly as snapping a piece of chocolate and the rocks on each side of the break were forced out of alignment. One side dropped down or was pushed past the other to make a distinct joint in the rock called a fault. Fractures in the crust also released material from the hot interior of the Earth, in the form of volcanoes, lava flows or upwellings of molten magma which solidified before reaching the surface and was later exposed by erosion. The molten material cooled into igneous rocks, as they are called, such as granite and basalt. The latter forms hexagonal columns like those of the Giant's

Left : A coral atoll raises itself clear of the sea, giving shelter in the lagoon from Pacific storms and space for luxuriant vegetation

Causeway of Ireland and Fingal's Cave of the Hebrides. The pressure and heat evolved in the crustal movement had one further effect on the rocks. It altered their crystalline structure in a process called metamorphosis. Soft limestones became marble, muddy deposits turned into slate and sandstones into quartzite. Minerals, including the precious stones and metal ores, were formed, and often concentrated into narrow seams that can be seen running through the bedrock as coloured 'flow bands'.

The raw material of the coastline is, therefore, a mixture of igneous and sedimentary rocks. Because of their varied composition and hardness they are affected in different ways by the elements that mould them into our familiar shores. The actual position of the shoreline changes with the evolving climate and the movements of the earth. The melting of the ice sheets raised the sea level and flooded low-lying coasts, while movements of the earth's crust have caused both the raising and lowering of coastlines. The Roman port at Pozzuoli, for example, was flooded in the fifteenth century and was resurrected later. When a new stretch of land does come in contact with the sea, it is immediately subject to an unceasing onslaught which can wear away the hardest rocks.

The sea has several different properties which contribute to its massive efficiency as an erosion engine, and which must be explained before their effects on the coastline can be examined.

Waves are generated by the friction of the wind that plucks at the surface of the water. The size of the waves depends on the speed of the wind, the length of time it has been blowing and the distance over which it blows. In theory, the speed of the waves would equal the windspeed, if the wind blew steadily for long enough but, as a storm passes over, the wind changes direction and the new wind tends to flatten and slow the old waves. When the wind drops, the waves continue to spread out, like ripples spreading over the surface of a pond. Waves generated in a storm hundreds of kilometres out to sea can arrive at the shore when there is a flat calm. The surface is glossy smooth but it heaves in a slow swell and huge breakers crash onto the rocks.

The direction of the swell shows where the storm took place and in which direction the wind was then blowing. A change of wind direction sets up a new train of waves, so that the ship-borne meteorologist can get an impression of distant weather by studying the waves. However, it is no use watching waves breaking on the shore. A train of waves approaching at an angle bends on reaching the shallows because the waves slow

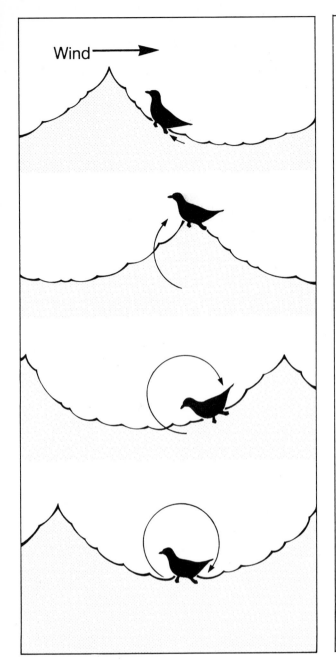

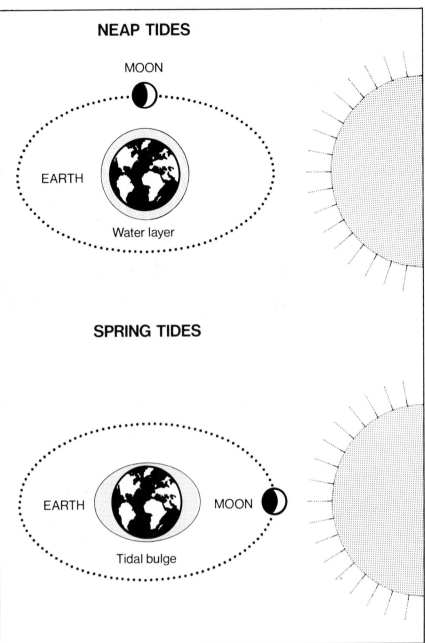

NEAP TIDES

MOON

EARTH

Water layer

SPRING TIDES

EARTH MOON

Tidal bulge

down in shallow water and then swing to break parallel to the shoreline. This is called refraction and can best be seen on a headland where the waves will break parallel to the shore on each side of it as well as at the head.

Several rough approximations can be made about the relation between wind and waves. Wave speed is roughly $\frac{3}{4}$ wind speed and the distance that a wave has travelled can also be calculated, though by a rather more complex equation. The most practical method of working out these quantities is the one devised by Admiral Beaufort, and the Beaufort Scale of wind speeds is used in every weather forecast.

There are other important aspects of wave movement which cannot be explained in terms of height, speed and distance. For example, when a wave breaks on the shore, the water is undoubtedly moving, yet a gull sitting in the open sea bobs up

and down, drifting only slightly with the waves. This is explained by a phenomenon called the wave orbit. Each drop of water at the surface is carried forward on the crest of the wave then rolls under in the trough, completing a circle in each wave cycle. The circle is not perfect, however, because of friction and there is a small forward movement of water which carries the gull with it. As the wave approaches a sloping shore, its advance meets with increasing resistance. When the sea is about one half the wave length deep, friction with the bottom distorts the wave orbit into an ellipse and at the bottom itself, the orbit is transformed into a to-and-fro movement. In clear water, seaweeds can be seen waving and sand grains are shuffled to leave ripple marks after the tide has gone out.

As the waves get closer to shore, they pile up, and the height increases while the wavelength

Above : Tides are produced by the pull of the Sun and Moon. The greatest tides, the springs, occur when Sun and Moon are in line. The smallest, the neaps, occur when Sun and Moon are at right angles and working in opposition
Above left : Waves are caused by wind moving across the sea. The water does not move with the waves, as is shown by the seabird whose forward movement is negligible

decreases. Friction at the bottom slows the water nearest to it, so the crest overhangs the trough until it finally topples over and breaks, forming a line of surf which hustles turbulently inshore. The water particles are now moving forwards instead of oscillating, and this is the point at which swimmers and boatmen risk getting engulfed in breaking waves and thrown ashore. There are two kinds of breaker. The plunging or combing breaker forms a hollow under the breaking crest just before it collapses. The spilling breaker breaks without a hollow forming and runs forward, pushing a strip of turbulent white water down its forward slope. The rush of water up the shore is called the swash. It loses momentum and runs back as the backwash or undertow.

The waves meet the land with an incredible release of pent-up energy. There may be a 100 ton force for every metre length of wave. A sloping beach gradually absorbs the energy over a wide front but on a vertical cliff enormous pressures are generated, eroding the cliff face and providing an especially rugged environment for the shore creatures.

There is a popular notion that every seventh wave is a giant. Observation will show that this is not true but there is no doubt that some waves are distinctly larger than others. This is due to the interaction of two or more trains of waves that have different speeds and wavelengths. A trough may cancel out a crest as the one train overtakes another or two crests may coincide to produce a monster wave.

The tidal waves that create havoc on unprotected coasts have nothing to do with tides. They are produced by earthquakes in the seabed and are better known by the Japanese name of *tsunami*. Tsunamis are less than a metre high and can be

Above : A desolate scene in a Norwegian fjord, an arm of the sea which penetrates deep into the mountains

barely detected in open water but they slowly pile up on sloping shores so that the ordinary wind-driven waves now break as much as ten metres (33 feet) higher than normal and extensive flooding results. In 1964, an earthquake destroyed Anchorage, Alaska, and generated tsunamis that reached California in nine hours and Australia in 20 hours, having travelled at a speed of 500 kilometres (310 miles) per hour.

The most obvious difference between a marine shore and that of an inland lake is that the seashore is subjected to tidal action that alternately covers and uncovers it, and thus has a profound effect on the animals that live there. Although tides work to a rhythm, their movements are by no means simple because they vary with time of year and from place to place. The basic tidal rhythm is a cycle of rise and fall taking place twice daily. Each cycle lasts approximately 12½

hours, so high and low water will be a little later each day. The distance that the water's edge moves vertically up and down the shore is the tidal range. On the American Gulf Coast the range is 0.3–0.6 metres (1–2 feet) but it is 2.5–6.0 metres (8–20 feet) in New England. Similarly, the Bristol Channel of western England has 12 metres (39 feet) tides but the west coast of Scotland has a tidal range of only 1.5 metres (5 feet). The Baltic and Mediterranean Seas are virtually tideless. On the other hand the Port of Southampton has four tides a day, two coming up each arm of the Solent.

Tides are caused by the gravitational attraction of the moon pulling the ocean waters towards it. Therefore, the form of tides varies throughout the 29½ day lunar month. The sun also affects tides so that when moon and sun are in line with the earth, they combine to produce larger than

Above: Sand-dunes invade a Brazilian river delta. In the distance a longshore current has created a sandbar diverting the course of the river

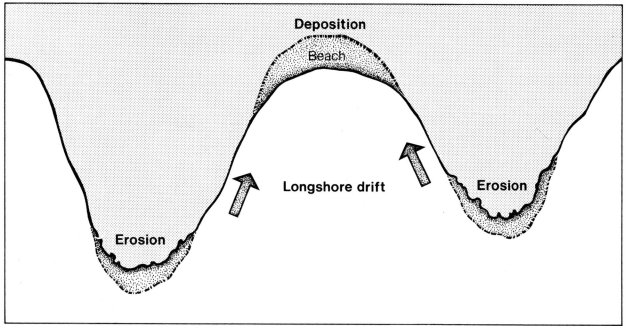

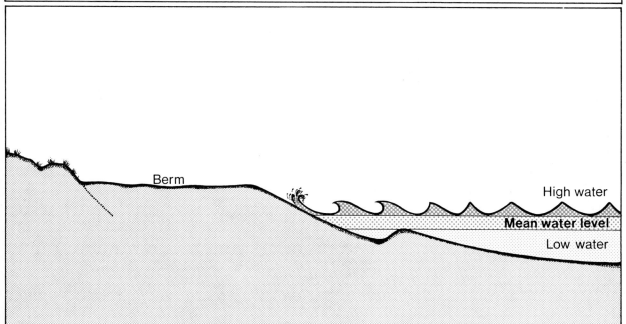

average tides, called the spring tides. During 'springs', as they are known, high tides are higher and low tides are lower than normal. They occur a little after full and new moons. When the moon, earth and sun form a right angle, as during the first and third quarters of the moon, the moon and sun work in opposition to produce neap tides which have a less than average range.

The tidal rhythm is further complicated by the fact that neither the moon's orbit around the earth, nor the earth's orbit around the sun is a perfect circle. At some times the moon comes closer to the earth than others so that its pull is greater and tidal range is increased at spring tides and decreased at neap tides. Finally, there comes a time when the moon is near the earth and the earth is near the sun, so the pull of both heavenly bodies is at a maximum. This happens twice a year, at the equinoxes of March and September, to produce the year's greatest tides. So the tidal range at any one spot is continually changing as moon, earth and sun circle around each other. The height of the moon above the horizon, its declination, also affects tides, and once in about 1600 years all three heavenly bodies are so placed to make the greatest possible tidal range. The last time this occurred was in the seventeenth century and the result was the catastrophic flooding of large parts of Holland. Villages were washed away and, even now, the flat landscape bears traces of the inundation.

The part of the shore which is covered and uncovered by the tides is called the littoral zone or foreshore. The upper reaches are uncovered by the tide for longer periods than the lower stretches but the length of exposure varies from day to day because of the changes in tidal range. The positions of the high and low tidemarks are continually

changing. Because the amount of exposure to air is, as we shall see, a very important factor in the life of seashore plants and animals, the littoral zone has been divided into a number of sections.

The mid-tide mark, the centre point around which the tides ebb and flow, is called Mean Sea Level. During neap tides, the rise and fall is small and the average tidemarks for the year are designated Mean High Water Neaps and Mean Low Water Neaps. Within these limits, animals and plants will always be covered and uncovered in one tidal cycle. Over the course of a fortnight, the neap tide range extends to spring tides to give two more tidemarks: Mean High and Low Water Springs. Between Mean High Springs and Mean High Neaps, animals and plants may go for several days without wetting and between Mean Low Neaps and Mean Low Springs they are similarly immersed continuously. Beyond in either direction are the Extreme High and Low Water Springs which are the limits of the equinoctial tides.

Both waves and tides produce currents along the shore which play an important part in forming the coastline. We have seen that waves making an oblique approach to a shore are refracted so that they finally run straight in. However, their final approach is not exactly parallel with the shoreline and the breaking wave sweeps in at a slight angle so the swash pushes the pebbles or sand in front of it. The result is a drift of material along the shore. Strong winds also push water up the shore and the excess escapes by flowing along the coast in a current, called the longshore current. The net result is a creeping of shore material in the direction of the prevailing wind so that sand beaches tend to form in bays where material is eroded from the headlands and driven in by wave

action. Drift of material along a sandy shore to a wide bay causes the formation of a sandspit, which is a continuation of the beach into the bay. Eventually a bar may form to seal off the bay and turn it into a lagoon. On many beaches, particularly in holiday resorts, the movement is reduced by building rows of groynes or breakwaters which trap the sand. The effect of the drift can be seen by the accumulation of sand on the upstream sides of the groynes and its removal on the sheltered sides.

Tidal currents flow to and fro. The ebb current flows as the tide falls, and then there follows a period of slack water before the flood current starts. Tidal currents have little effect on open shores but they are important in estuaries and where the tide has to flow between islands. The Pentland Firth is the channel that runs between mainland Britain and the Orkney Islands, thereby linking the North Sea with the Atlantic Ocean. Tidal currents of 9 knots pour through the Firth as one sea empties into the other and in the process they bring navigation by small boats to a standstill.

The first stage in the formation of a new line of coast is the cutting of a small cliff where water meets land. Rock fragments gradually gather at the bottom of the cliff as a shingle beach. The fragments roll about in the waves to make rounded cobbles and pebbles or are fined down to sand and are dashed against the cliff to hasten its erosion. Where the bedrock is weaker, more rapid erosion forms gullies and caves while harder rock is left behind as a promontory or an isolated stack. Eventually sufficient shingle or sand accumulates as an abrasion platform that extends down the shore to absorb the waves' impact and protect the cliff from further destruction. Cobbles form

21

steep beaches and sands spread into shallow wide beaches. Because water filters through cobbles easily, there is virtually no backwash and the swash continually forces the cobbles up the shore. Soft cliffs may be continually eroded, as on the Norfolk coast of England or at Cape Cod where a single storm can cut the cliff several metres and send houses tumbling into the sea below.

Longshore drift of material can expose the coast to further erosion. Some places are notorious for erosion and artificial 'cliffs' in the form of concrete sea walls have to be built. The gentle regular waves of summer push sand up the shore to make a rampart at the back of a beach called a berm. The berm's surface lies beyond the reach of the tides and it may run into a sand dune system behind the shore. Winter gales, with short, steep waves, have a backwash more powerful than the swash and cut away the berm, but on a stable shore some berm is left and it regenerates during the following summer.

Tidal currents cause a to-and-fro flow of water in estuaries which, through the addition of water coming down the river, has a net seaward movement. Silt brought down by the river becomes clotted when it meets sea water and, along with sediments brought in by the sea, forms mudflats and sandbanks which are exposed at low tide.

The mud is gradually stabilized through colonization by such plants as the cord grass *Spartina*. The roots trap more mud and the mudflat gradually rises above high tide to become a salt marsh or salting. A whole succession of plant life is established as the mud rises from the sea. Eelgrass (*Zostera*) grows under water; glasswort (*Salicornia*) is submerged by the tide each day, whereas sea rush (*Juncus maritimis*) survives almost on dry land, needing only a few hours submergence each month. Hummocks of mud develop around the plants and gradually form islands separated by pools and channels or creeks through which the tide runs. The salt marsh will end abruptly at a salting cliff where there is a drop of one metre or less to the bare mudflat below.

Where there is no tidal or other current to scour the estuary, deposition of sediments continues unabated and various forms of delta result. The classical delta is that of the Nile whose triangular shape resembles the Greek letter *delta*. The drift of material along the coast gradually formed a series of bars with shallow lagoons behind, the broad estuary filled up with silt from the annual floods and the River Nile divided into a number of channels meandering through the bars. The River Seine has formed a delta in the shelter of a deep estuary, where drift cannot carry sediments away despite its position on the Atlantic seaboard of France. On the other side of the Atlantic, the Mississippi delta thrusts into the Gulf of Mexico. The river has no broad estuary but runs straight into a sheltered sea, depositing its load of sediment to form bars on each side. Over the years, the stream has meandered to left and right forming a promontory some 200 kilometres (125 miles) long. The river has several exits to the sea leaving a tangle of abandoned channels.

Present-day water requirements for crop irrigation, industry and household use have caused many of the world's rivers to be dammed at intervals along their courses. Material is held back behind the dams so that estuaries and adjacent beaches are starved of sediment. The Aswan Dam on the Nile is already causing the disappearance of beaches around its delta and the same is happening around the Gulf of Mexico. With the disappearance of the beaches and mudflats comes a disappearance of marine life and disaster for fishermen who depend on these waters for a living.

Around the warmer seas of the world, there is a form of seashore quite unlike any other. Other shores accumulate from material gathering by physical processes, but coral reefs accumulate through the growth of animals and plants. The most important of these are the coral animals, which are related to the sea anemones, but these are assisted by other animals and by certain algae related to the corallines of temperate shores. All the coral organisms lay down hard skeletons, usually of lime, which persist long after the animal or plant has died and so accumulate to form huge masses. The true or stony corals may lead independent lives, or several individuals may be joined to form a colony. These are the main reef builders and they are joined by horny corals, also known as sea fans or gorgonians, of which the Mediterranean precious coral (*Corallium rubrum*) is an example. There are also soft corals, which include the organpipe coral (*Tubipora musica*), dead man's fingers (*Alcyonium*) and sea pens (*Pennatulacea*). The true corals, which are pink or purple, are classified by their shape, as for instance the brain corals (*Meandrina*) and stag's-horn corals (*Acropora*). Another major constituent of the reef is a relative, the stinging coral *Millipora*, which is quite unpleasant to touch.

Not all coral animals build reefs, indeed two species of true coral live in rock pools in southwest Britain. Reefs are only found in waters warmer than 18°C (64°F). The water must be quite shallow, less than 85 metres (280 feet) deep,

Below : Accessories of a coral reef ; dead man's fingers and stinging coral add exotic form and colour

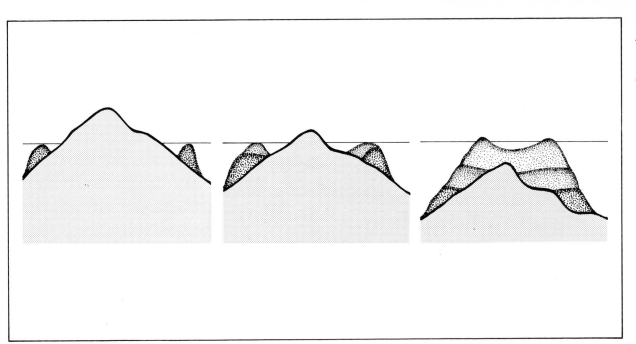

Left: A coral atoll is formed around a sunken volcanic island. As the island slowly sinks, a fringing circlet of coral grows up in the shallow water

and free of mud. There are three main kinds of reef: fringing, barrier and atolls.

Fringing reefs build up as platforms running parallel to the shore, and up to 2.5 km (1½ miles) wide. Coral formation is strongest in front of headlands and facing the prevailing winds where the cleanest water is to be found. The force of the waves is broken by steep gullies, or surge channels, which funnel water onto the reef, and by boilers, mushroom-shaped heads of corals which have grown closely together so that waves pass between the 'mushroom stalks' and foam out of gaps between the heads.

Breaks in the reef occur opposite river mouths where the water is thick and muddy, an important pointer for ships trying to seek shelter in the lagoon behind the reef. Barrier reefs form on a larger scale. Running 15–160 kilometres (10–100 miles) offshore, they may be many kilometres wide and over 2000 kilometres (1250 miles) long. Atolls are circular coral masses found particularly in the tropical Pacific. They are the coral islands of romantic stories and rise from the ocean depths with no attachment to land masses. The lagoon inside is shallow but, outside, the bottom descends steeply to the ocean floor. There are several possible ways in which atolls have been formed. Charles Darwin suggested that the reef formed around a volcano which has since subsided into the sea. Subsidence was slow so that reef formation was able to keep pace with it. Vindication for this idea came from borings into Eniwetok Atoll in the Marshall Islands of the Pacific. These showed that 1300 metres (4300 feet) of coral reef were resting on a volcanic foundation. Subsidence of the volcano and raising of the reef has taken 50 million years.

Coral reefs frequently show above water at low tide and the pulverizing of coral in storms can produce sand which forms beaches and low islands called cays. Cays are frequently swamped in storms and are short of fresh water but they have been settled by islanders who subsist on coconut palms, which survive in brackish water, and on fish caught in the lagoons.

The Margins of the Sea

The seashore is the frontier between two realms. It is a disputed zone between the sea and the land, where the fortunes of each side ebb and flow with the tides. At high tide the shore is marine. Fishes swim in, sea anemones and fanworms unfold to feed, and every variety of animal sheds eggs and sperms into the sea. When the tide drops many animals have to retreat into deeper water but others can stay where they are. Limpets clamp to the rock face and crabs bury themselves in moist sand. For a while the shore joins forces with the land. Birds alight to poke among rocks and probe into sand. Lizards, rats and foxes come down to forage, and on Scottish islands even sheep and chickens find a living there.

On this shifting frontier, the marine element is dominant. The animals and plants of the shore have their roots in the sea. They are moving towards a terrestrial existence but, for one reason or another, have not been able to sever links with the sea completely. Many spend their early life afloat before settling on the shore. By comparison, very few organisms are moving in the opposite direction. Not many terrestrial species are capable of withstanding inundation by sea water. A few flowering plants, a handful of insects and the marine iguana of the Galapagos Islands are usually all that will be found on these shores. We should not forget, perhaps, that the sea snakes,

Right: Rocky beaches, here on the Pribilof Islands of Alaska, are made slippery by fronds of brown seaweed

turtles, seals and whales are the descendants of land animals which have made a permanent home in the sea, although the turtles, seals and some of the sea snakes have to return to land for breeding.

The basically marine animals and plants found on the shore may be tied to the sea, yet they represent a striving to escape a marine existence. They form only a small proportion of marine species, the tip of an iceberg, the bulk of which is still submerged. A swim below the low spring tide mark will reveal the bulk of the iceberg. Otherwise a close examination of a tide pool will suffice. This behind-the-lines area is the home of animals that cannot stand exposure on the shore for more than a brief moment. Starfish, sea urchins and brittlestars, sea squirts and sponges, myriads of little fishes, octopuses, scallops, whelks and oysters, spider crabs and even lobsters are all to be found in pools and under rocks. Many of these will be familiar to the beach visitor because their remains are often cast up on the shore after a storm, but if we are tied to the shore, these animals are tantalizingly out of reach and to see them through a mask or in a pool should remind us that we only see a shore when it is not at its best. At low tide, everything has shut up shop; but at high tide seaweeds float in inverted curtains, crabs scuttle, limpets and periwinkles wander slowly over the rocks as these marine species enjoy what is their true element.

Necessity forces us to study the shore at low tide when it is not always possible to watch the behaviour of its inhabitants. However, if the inhabitants are hidden or inert, evidence of various physical factors influencing shore life is there for all to see. This evidence only becomes significant if the position of the shore as a boundary zone where the marine environment grades into dry land is clearly put into perspective. It must be remembered that the oceans and seas are immense. They cover over two-thirds of the world's surface and are over 10 kilometres (6 miles) deep in places. Yet the sea is a remarkably constant environment for life when compared with the land. The hottest tropical waters are 35°C (90°F), whereas a desert surface can have a daily temperature range of 30°–50°C (86–122°F). Polar sea water drops to no more than −1.9°C (28°F) but midwinter temperatures on the Antarctic coastline drop to −40°C (−40°F). Nowhere does the water temperature fluctuate widely or rapidly and animals can adapt easily to any small changes they may meet.

Similarly, there is great stability in the chemical composition of sea water. Sodium chloride – common salt – makes up nearly 80 per cent of the

Above : Larger life of the seashore. On the tropical Galapagos Islands, marine iguanas bask in the sun. They are loathe to change their warm berths for the relatively cold water even if chased

soluble salts in sea water. The salt concentration, or salinity, is expressed in parts per thousand rather than as a percentage. It ranges from 43 parts per thousand in the Red Sea where the salts are concentrated by the evaporation of water to 7 parts per thousand in the Baltic Sea where sea water is diluted by fresh water from rivers. The average for open oceans is 35 parts per thousand.

A constant salinity is essential for marine animals; any sudden change can be fatal because of the phenomenon of osmosis. This is the tendency of water to move through a semi-permeable barrier from a low salt concentration on one side to a high concentration on the other. Tissues of animals and plants are made up of cells which have semi-permeable walls, that is they allow the passage of water but not of salts. The salinity of sea water is roughly the same as the salt concentration in the cells of most marine animals so not much water flows in or out. Any major change in the salinity of sea water will disrupt the balance between sea water and body fluids. The animal will shrivel or inflate as water is sucked out or drawn in, or as the kidneys race to drain off excess water they also throw out the vital salts.

Animals with a land ancestry have a salt concentration in their tissues lower than that of sea water so they face the problem of losing body water to the sea when immersed. The majority of fishes, excluding the sharks and their relatives, have returned to the sea from fresh water during the course of evolution. They have to replace water that has been sucked out of their bodies through osmosis by drinking, literally like a fish. As their drinking water is salt, their kidneys have to work hard to get rid of the excess. The sharks bolster the salt concentration in their blood with urea, a product of the body chemistry that is usually excreted through the kidneys. This keeps the body fluids level with the sea water outside and there is little passage of water.

Equable temperature and salinity make the sea a good place to live in but animals also need food and oxygen for survival. As on land, all animals ultimately depend on plants for food. Plants obtain nourishment from nitrate and phosphate salts and get their energy from the sun. The sun's energy is collected by the process of photosynthesis which combines carbon dioxide and water into carbohydrates. Marine plants, therefore, need certain salts and gases and sunlight. There is no shortage of carbon dioxide and oxygen in the sea and nutrient salts are liberated by the decomposition of dead animals and plants. Light is the main limiting factor to plant growth.

Below: The polar bear of the Arctic is not worried by freezing temperatures when it hunts for fish, but will find little else on the shore in winter to satisfy its appetite

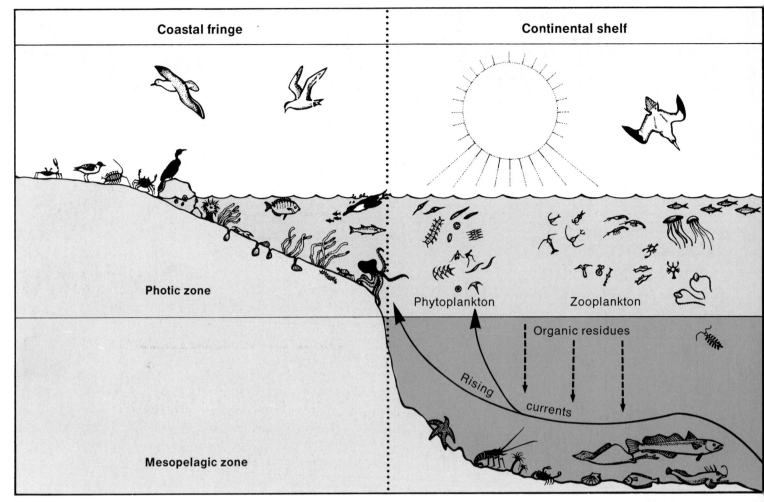

Photic zone

Phytoplankton   Zooplankton

Organic residues

Rising

currents

Mesopelagic zone

Ninety per cent of the oceans' mass is pitch dark because sunlight is reflected at the surface and, even in crystal clear water, there is barely enough light for photosynthesis at depths of more than 20–30 metres (66–98 feet).

The well-lit upper layer of the sea is called the photic zone. Most marine life is concentrated there, the basis of all this life being masses of microscopic plants, such as dinoflagellates and diatoms. Each one is too small to be seen with the naked eye but the sum of all these minute plants makes an enormous mass of living material, perhaps ten tons to each acre. The plants drift helplessly, 'fixing' the sun's energy by photosynthesis and providing food for swarms of small animals, crustaceans, baby fishes as well as for the larvae of many kinds of invertebrate animals. The passive nature of these plants and animals earns them the general name of plankton, from the Greek for 'that which floats'. The planktonic animals, zooplankton, having harvested the crop of minute plants, the phytoplankton, become the food of larger animals, from pilchards to blue whales. When they die, their bodies decompose and the constituents are liberated to feed the phytoplankton again. The whole system of life can be thought of as a never-ending cycle of life powered by the sun's energy.

Compared with the equable nature of the ocean, the seashore is a place of contrasts. It well deserves the simile of a battle-scarred no man's land. Being a transitional zone between land and sea it is exposed to opposing forces. Waves travel hundreds of miles unchecked and, although they have little effect in open water, smash against the coastline subjecting anything they hit to huge pressures. Boulders, ships and bathers are dashed about – and it is surprising that anything animate can survive this remorseless pounding. Shores exposed to the open ocean are, not surprisingly, rather bare and a storm always leaves a line of torn weeds and broken shells but even on the most exposed coast some plants and animals will survive the worst storm.

Salinity changes are not a problem for shore animals unless then live in an estuary or are subjected to heavy rainfall at low tide, when a soaking in fresh water could be disastrous. Temperature is a stiffer problem at low tide when the sheltering blanket of water is withdrawn. A paddle along the shore shows that shallow water is considerably warmer than deep water and, once exposed, the sand and rocks soon warm up under a clear, sunny sky. Despite their vulnerability the inhabitants can survive the normal range of temperatures. There are some tropical oysters

Above : Each region of the sea has its own community of animals. In the open sea there is a cycle of life with sunlight inducing a bloom of animals and plants at the surface. Once dead, their bodies sink and decay. Rising currents carry the products of decomposition to fertilize further generations. Shorelife also benefits from the nutrients and dead animals washed in

which can survive body temperatures of as much as 45°C (113°F). Abnormal weather, however, may be fatal, as on the coast of southern California where a persistent cold wind sometimes kills the seaweeds.

Together with the ability to withstand the pounding of waves, the most obviously necessary characteristic of shore life is resistance to drying-up. All inhabitants of the shore must, by definition of 'the shore', be exposed to desiccation. Those living at the upper end of the shore are exposed to the air for longer periods than those near the low-tide mark and must have progressed farther towards a terrestrial way of life. Some animals and plants can withstand a physical drying of their tissues, and their bodies will lose an amount of water that is fatal to other species. This is a physiological adaptation to desiccation. The alternative is to avoid dessication. Limpets clamp to the rock to make a watertight fit. Barnacles and bivalves close their shells and many animals hide under stones or bury themselves in sand and mud, where a high humidity prevails throughout the period of exposure. Because animals and plants on the shore differ in their ability to resist dessication they are sorted into zones of distribution up the shore. This zonation from top to bottom of the shore is the most obvious feature of intertidal life and is so important that it forms the framework for all discussion of the natural history of shores.

The Ecology of the Shore

Before the distribution of animals and plants into zones is elaborated, the shore should be considered as a biological unit in the same way as the open sea has been described. To understand the individual life of a single plant or animal properly it has to be considered as a part of the shore community. The animal or plant may be beautifully suited to a small corner of the shore environment but it does not live in isolation. A balance is maintained between individuals of the same species and between that species and other members of the community. There is competition for food and living space and the balance between co-existing species can be affected by physical factors. For example, on open coasts knotted wrack (*Ascophyllum nodosum*) prefers sheltered places and anchors itself to large boulders, while bladder wrack (*Fucus vesiculosus*) takes more exposed sites and may anchor to small stones that are unsuitable for knotted wrack.

The actual composition of the shore community depends on the shore's exposure to wave action, the nature of the shore in the form of boulders, open rock, sand or mud, and the interactions

Above: A Sally Lightfoot crab feasts on a stranded jellyfish; animals and plants thrown up from the deep are important food supplies for shore animals

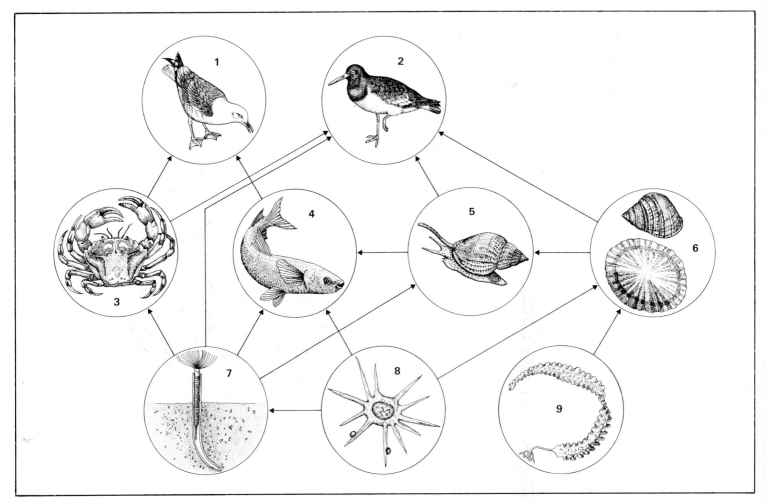

between the animals and plants present. There is a cycle of life on the shore which, as in the open sea, is powered by the sun's energy being trapped by the photosynthesis of plants. Animals eat the plants acquiring the stored energy and are eaten in turn so there is a 'food chain' in which energy is transferred from one organism to another. Because they are the first link in the chain, plants are called primary producers. The animals that eat them, such as limpets, periwinkles and sand-hoppers, are herbivores or primary consumers. Predatory animals that eat the herbivores are carnivores or secondary consumers. They include crabs, whelks, starfish and many small fishes, which are themselves eaten by the top carnivores or tertiary consumers such as gulls and oyster-catchers.

Of the energy fixed by photosynthesis, only a fraction reaches the top carnivores. At each stage of the food chain energy is being used up by the bodily activities of the organisms. Energy is used up in respiration, to drive muscular contractions, and to power digestion and reproduction. Energy is also wasted because of the inefficiencies of the digestive processes. Herbivores absorb only about ten per cent of the energy of the plants they eat; the rest passes through the system. For this reason there must always be fewer animals in the higher links of the food chain. There are more periwinkles than whelks that eat them. This is, however, a simplification. At any one time there may be fewer prey animals on the shore than there are predators eating them. The paradox is resolved by the rapid breeding rate of the prey. The 'standing crop' of prey animals, which can be imagined as the stock in the larder, is replaced as fast as the predators can eat it.

The net result of the food chain is a dissipation of energy at each link. If a plant or animal is not eaten, probably a rare occurrence except in the case of the top carnivores, it is broken down at death by bacteria and its energy released. The food chain is, therefore, continually losing energy, but the loss is made good by the plants on the shore trapping energy from sunlight and there are extra sources which help to make the shore a particularly rich place. At each tide, the water floods over the shore, bringing with it phyto-plankton which can be captured by herbivores like mussels and cockles that strain the minute plants from the water. It also brings organic debris ranging from torn-up shreds of seaweed to dead whales. In whatever form, the debris finds hungry mouths ready for it.

The idea of a food chain is itself a simplification. It is true that periwinkles eat seaweed and are

Above: A simplified food web shows the relations between these typical seashore predators and prey:
1 gull; 2 oystercatcher; 3 crab; 4 mullet; 5 whelk; 6 periwinkle and limpet; 7 tubeworm; 8 plankton; 9 seaweed. Ultimately, all animal life depends on plants but, like all ecological communities, shorelife is linked in a series of interrelationships. The arrows show how the 'food' progresses up the web to the birds – the tertiary consumers – at the top

eaten by whelks, which are, in their turn, eaten by gulls, but the relationship of eater and eaten is much more complex than a linear chain. Most animals on the shore, if not all, have varied diets. There is an almost bewildering variety of food chains and it is better to talk of a 'food web' to describe all the links. As a relatively simple example of a web, the food chain described above can be expanded by fitting extra links. Gulls, the top carnivores, eat periwinkles, so leaving out the carnivore or secondary consumer stage. Gulls also eat other herbivores, such as mussels, barnacles and limpets, as well as many carnivores like crabs, fishes and starfishes. To complicate matters further, some gulls eat other top carnivores. They steal the eggs and nestlings of other birds and even of their own species. When all the animals on the shore are linked together as prey and predators, the web becomes at least as complicated as the wiring of a telephone exchange.

The complexity of interactions between members of a food web can be demonstrated by considering what might happen if one member is removed. Suppose Man, at the top of the chain, decides to harvest periwinkles. He wants to appropriate as many as he can for his own use so he shoots any gull he sees on the shore. But the periwinkle population does not rise in response to the removal of gulls because gulls also eat crabs and whelks which flourish and so eat more periwinkles. A practical example of this came to light when British cockle fishermen complained that oystercatchers were competing for their cockles and wanted them shot. Despite an outcry many oystercatchers were shot, and all to no avail because competition for cockles was not limited to Man and oystercatcher. Flatfish are much more important as predators of cockles in the sandy bays where the fisheries are based, so any effect the birds might have had on cockle numbers was masked by the depredations of flatfish. Even if it was possible to exterminate all flatfish, cockle numbers might well be held in check by the amount of food available for their own consumption.

Scientific studies of seashore concentrate on two major aspects: the distribution of the animals and plants on the shore, mainly in respect to exposure to waves and air, and the untangling of the food web. Studying food webs requires sophisticated techniques, particularly if the study is to be taken to its ultimate: describing the links of the chains in terms of precise measurement of energy transfer. At a simpler level it is easier to work out the diet of a particular animal and to study its feeding habits to show its position in the

Below: Seaweeds are gathered on the coast of Brittany to be strewn on the fields as a manure

shore's economy. The study of the distribution of flora and fauna is quite simple. Anyone following the tide will notice that particular species of animals and plants are uncovered at certain tide levels. It soon becomes clear that the shore is divided into a series of well-defined zones. All that is necessary to discover the zonation of a particular shore is a knowledge of the commoner species present there. This study is made easier because the same basic zonation is found throughout the world. This should not, of course, discourage anyone from the close study of a particular shore, for each one is subtly different from any other and there remain, in any case, unresolved questions about the exact nature of shore zonation.

The Divisions of the Shore

Zones of plants and animals succeed one another in strips that run horizontally along the shore from land to seaward edges. Every shore has its zonation, even in landlocked almost tideless seas, but the zonation on muddy or sandy beaches is obscured because most animals live under the surface at low tide. Here, we will consider the rocky shore with a good tidal range.

The clearest zonations are on steep cliff faces or seawalls where a casual glance shows a conspicuous striping. At about the half-tide mark, the rocks are whitened by a sheet of barnacles. Below the barnacles are dense fronds of seaweed, while above them the rocks are blackened with a film of lichen, which conceals the periwinkles sheltering in crevices. This particular pattern of zonation is just one of almost infinite possibilities. There are probably as many patterns as there are shores in the world, because zonation is the result of a number of factors, of which tide, exposure to

Left : The shore is a shifting frontier between land and sea, Seawards from the splash zone, there are a series of zones, each increasingly influenced by the sea, as it is uncovered by low tide for a shorter period than the one above

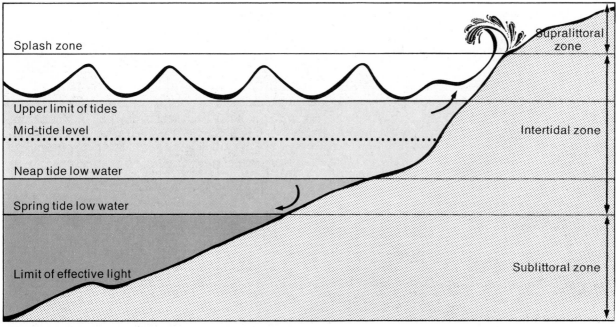

Splash zone

Supralittoral zone

Upper limit of tides

Mid-tide level

Intertidal zone

Neap tide low water

Spring tide low water

Limit of effective light

Sublittoral zone

the open sea and the topography of the shore are the most important.

Shelving shores do not have such a neat zonation, but it exists nonetheless. Owing to the shallow angle of the land, the strips of animals and seaweeds are much larger in area, although the vertical distance of each corresponds to that on the cliff face. The zonation is also complicated by the irregularities of the shore, where pools of water and boulders distort the orderly progress from low to high tide marks.

Despite the variety of shore zones round the world, they all share a basic pattern. After a world-wide study, Professor T. A. Stephenson divided rocky shores into three major biological zones: the supralittoral fringe, the midlittoral zone and the sublittoral fringe.

The supralittoral fringe lies at the top of the shore, above all but the highest tides, and its inhabitants are wetted mainly by rain and spray. In fine weather, the zone may become bone dry for the fortnight between successive spring tides. Below this stretches the broad expanse of the midlittoral zone which is covered and uncovered regularly at almost every tide in the year. The sublittoral fringe is above water only at the lowest spring tides and, even then, is barely exposed long enough for the water to run off and the rocks to dry. Below the shore, the sublittoral zone extends out to sea. It is never uncovered but nevertheless differs from the seabed farther out because it is affected by wave action.

These three major zones of the shore have their characteristic inhabitants. The supralittoral fringe presents a rather barren prospect and its common animals are the sea slater, the nautical relative of the woodlice, a few insects and the small periwinkle. After a storm, the fringe is enriched

*Above : Rocky outcrops
on a sandy beach
provide anchorages for
seaweeds which are
exposed at every tide
Right : At the top of
the beach, sea slaters
feed on seaweeds that
have been torn and cut
up by the waves*

by a line of dead seaweed which gives food and shelter to a host of land and shore animals. The rocks will probably be stained black by lichens and, if the surface is suitable, there will be splashes of orange lichen and flowering plants such as thrift (*Armeria maritima*). The boundary between supralittoral zone and midlittoral fringe is marked by the sudden appearance of barnacles. Indeed, barnacles may be the only species present although they are often joined by periwinkles, limpets and seaweeds. Nearer the sea, beds of mussels oust the barnacles and dogwhelks wander in search of prey. Anemones live in crevices on the lower shore, where, at low tide, they pull their tentacles into their mouths. They survive in shady places through the reservoir of water held in their hollow bodies.

The sublittoral zone is marked by the edge of the 'forest' of tangleweed whose stout stems and broad fronds, so much like a slimy razor-strop, become a hazard to boatman and swimmer as well as to anyone trying to find a footing on the rocks. The rocks here may also have a covering of pink corallines. These are algae whose bodies are impregnated with lime and are not to be confused with corals, which are animals with limy skeletons. These coralline-encrusted stones make attractive ornaments when dried.

The three major zones of any rock shore make a framework on which the zonation of other plants and animals can be imposed. Each species occupies a greater or lesser stretch of shore depending on its ability to survive the exacting conditions of the shore environment. Biologists are by no means agreed on what decides the zonation of many species. The problem can be studied by recording the position of a particular organism on a variety of shores. Change in the physical condition of the shore may be reflected in the incidence and positioning of the organism and so give a clue as to what is affecting it. Laboratory experiments may then confirm the limits of tolerance and hence the zoning. If we are lucky, we can then see what character in the animal's anatomy or physiology prevents it from spreading farther up or down the shore.

Barnacles, for instance, have definite boundaries on a vertical face, above and below which they do not survive. The boundaries must mark some limiting factor. Barnacles are crustaceans, relatives of shrimps and crabs despite their outward resemblance to limpets. They start life as minute larvae that swim just below the sea's surface. When the time comes to settle, the larva starts to search for a suitable home. Its preference for swimming at the surface ensures that it is swept

Above: Seashore animals must avoid drying up at low tide. These barnacles close the operculum of their shells

right up the shore where it can test the rock surface. The larva seeks the traces that departed barnacles have left behind them. This leads it to settle among other barnacles, a sure sign of a favourable site. The larva lands on its head, glues itself to the rock, grows a protective suit of armour and spends the rest of its life using its legs to sweep food into its mouth. However, a gregarious tendency does not explain why the swarm of barnacles should not spread beyond these limits. Many larvae fail to find a suitable home and perish. There must be something wrong with the environment outside the strict limits of the barnacle zone.

It seems the upper limit is set by the length of time the barnacles are uncovered and exposed to drying up and overheating. If there are cool, shady crevices, the barnacles can establish themselves farther up the shore. On the other front, barnacles are ousted from the lower shore by settlements of mussels and wracks, and probably by the attacks of predators. The influence of wracks can be seen where an isolated frond has cleared an area of barnacles by its constant movement in the waves.

The Tides and their Influence
Not surprisingly, the movement of the tides has

the largest effect on zonation. Any plant or animal uncovered by the falling tide is exposed to a two-fold danger of drying up and also overheating or freezing. The period of time that they are at risk depends on their position on the beach. At the Low Water Springs level the shore is exposed for four per cent of the year, so animals and plants here are uncovered for only a few hours every fortnight. At Low Water Neaps, only a metre or so up the shore, exposure has risen to 20 per cent and at High Water Neaps, the shore is uncovered for 80 per cent of the time.

On rocky shores, periwinkles range from the splash zone, where only spray from the worst storms reaches, to the lowest margins of the shore. They are particulary interesting because they appear to be making the transition from sea to land, and the zonation of the species shows an increasing ability to live out of water. Some periwinkles actually drown if kept immersed in water. The small periwinkle (*Littorina neritoides*) ranges from the topmost part of the shore, up to 7.6 metres (25 feet) above the highest tide, down to the middle of the barnacle belt, and it meets the rough periwinkle (*Littorina saxatilis*) in the lowest parts of the splash zone. The third species, the flat periwinkle (*Littorina littoralis*) is confined to the zone of wracks which provide it

Below : A rock pool takes on the appearance of a garden with branching and encrusting coralline seaweeds and green sea lettuce

with shelter and food. The common or edible periwinkle (*Littorina littorea*) is the largest, being sufficiently large and abundant to be worth harvesting. It extends down to Low Water Springs but also mingles with other periwinkles up to High Water Neaps.

The zonation of these four European species is based on their ability to withstand drying and warming. Periwinkles are provided with a trap-door, the operculum, which seals the opening of the shell when the animal has retreated inside. The operculum prevents water loss but it also stops the periwinkle from breathing. The small peri-winkle survives high on the beach because it can shut down its body activities and keep the shell closed for a long time. Specimens have survived as long as five months without water by conserving water and cutting down respiration.

Other species have to open the operculum to breathe. As soon as they do this they begin to lose water. In one experiment, all small peri-winkles survived seven days at 18°C (64°F), whereas 80 per cent of flat periwinkles and 70 per cent of common periwinkles died. Heat itself can be fatal. At a certain temperature, periwinkles go into a 'heat coma', when the operculum opens and the animal dries up rapidly. Again, the small periwinkle does not go into a coma until its temperature has risen to 40°C (104°F), whereas the flat periwinkle cannot survive temperatures of 30°C (86°F) and has to seek the shade of wracks at low tide.

The common periwinkle at the bottom of the shore lays its eggs in spring. As the tide rises, the female sheds her eggs in capsules. Each egg hatches into a small, floating larva which turns into a tiny snail when two or three months old. This is a life-style adopted by many sea animals.

Above left: Colourful rough periwinkles survive exposure by sheltering in a damp crevice near the top of the shore

Thus adult starfish, sea-urchins, barnacles and shellfish have little or no powers of locomotion but their free-floating larvae can spread over a wide area and aid the distribution of the species. The system is, however, very costly for the species. The majority of the larvae fail to find a suitable settling place and perish. A female barnacle lays thousands of eggs at a time but only two in every thousand successfully establish themselves on a rock. Losses for shore animals are particularly high because they can survive only in a narrow zone. The mortality rate of these animals can be reduced by omitting the hazardous larval stage. The flat periwinkle lays its eggs on wracks and they hatch into baby snails. The rough periwinkle goes further. It retains the eggs in its body and actually gives birth to baby snails.

Perversely, the small periwinkle living at the top of the shore has reversed this trend and still retains marine breeding habits. The adult is, to all intents, a land animal breathing air instead of extracting oxygen from water with gills, and surviving long periods without water. Yet its eggs are laid in the sea and hatch into floating larvae. Egg-laying takes place during the winter spring tides when the periwinkles are most likely to be submerged. The larvae cannot expect to establish themselves among their parents in the high splash zone and instead settle among the barnacles lower down, before crawling up the shore above the tidemark.

The wracks are tough fronded brown algae which are moored to rocks by a 'holdfast'. On many shores they form a carpet over the rocks from the highest tidemark and disappear into the sea beyond the littoral zone. The carpet looks lifeless but the fronds are important as a damp, cool shelter for many animals. A sheltered shore

Above : Channel wrack, a brown seaweed, can dry to a black crisp and recover when the tide returns

39

will have a range of half a dozen or more brown seaweeds, each taking its appropriate place on the shore. On a typical British shore, which has equivalents the world over, the highest brown weeds are channel wrack (*Pelvetia*) and, overlapping slightly, spiral wrack (*Fucus spiralis*) which lives in the upper barnacle and lower winkle zone. These two are resistant to dessication because their small fronds have a small surface area for the loss of water. Channel wrack survives complete drying up at neap tides. Its fronds become black and crisp but they revive on wetting and quickly regain their suppleness.

The channel and spiral wrack zone is replaced in midshore by bladder wrack and knotted wrack. Both are distinguished by the round bladders and they are the seaweeds which are supposed to forecast the weather, by the bladders bursting with a 'pop' if the weather is going to be fine. The explanation is that dry bladders rupture explosively when squeezed between the fingers. When wet they just squelch. Their true function is to buoy the fronds when submerged so that the carpet of wrack becomes a swaying forest through which fishes and prawns swim. Below the bladder-bearing species comes saw wrack (*Fucus serratus*), which may mingle with them at the zone's boundary.

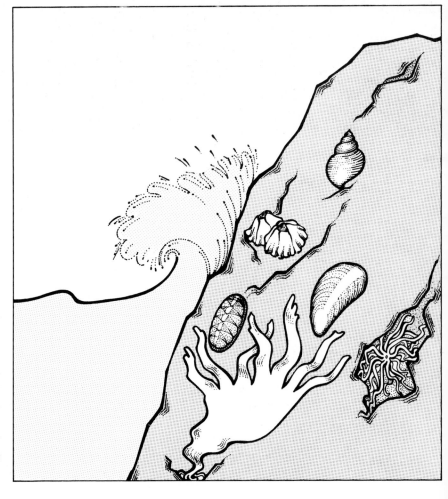

40

The growth of these wracks is dependent on the time spent uncovered by the tide. Spiral wrack, for instance, grows best when subjected to wetting and drying in six hourly bouts, but serrated wrack cannot survive such a regime. It needs 11 hours soaking in every 12 and dies if exposed for 11 hours.

The sublittoral fringe sees the wracks replaced by larger brown algae. There is the thongweed (*Himanthalia elongata*) whose long, thin fronds grow from a button-shaped base, and fan-shaped peacock's-tail (*Padina pavonia*). At the lowest levels, exposed only briefly at spring tides, there are the big tangles of oarweeds. *Laminaria saccharina* has a 6 metres (20 feet) long frond and *Laminaria digitata* receives its scientific name from the frond that divides into fingers. Paralleling the brown weeds' zonation, the shore will have changing populations of red and green algae. These are less conspicuous than the browns but prove on close examination to be delicate and often beautifully formed.

The tide's influence on zonation is modified by the topography and geology of the shore, and by interactions between the animals and plants. In technical books the term 'exposure of the shore' usually means exposure to wave action rather than exposure to air. The fauna and flora of a shore is largely determined by the amount of shelter from the force of incoming waves. Waves can knock animals from the rock and tear algae from their moorings. There is often a considerable difference between the zonation on each side of a headland that projects across the prevailing run of the sea. The sheltered side of the headland or the recesses of a deep bay will contain species that cannot withstand wave action. Knotted wrack, for example, is replaced by bladder wrack in less sheltered places and both disappear on wave-exposed rocks, leaving the surface clear for barnacles. On the other hand, small periwinkles like exposed situations because they will receive plenty of spray and the purple laver (*Porphyria umbicalis*) seems to like the lack of competition from other algae. On American coasts, rocky shores exposed to the full pounding of the surf are inhabited by the purple starfish *Pisaster*, which only a jemmy will prise from its anchorage, and the purple urchin *Strongylocentrus purpuratus* which digs a pit in the rock so that it cannot be dislodged.

On tropical shores, Sally Lightfoot crabs run about on exposed rocks. They survive the pounding of the waves by gripping the rock with their sharp claws, and their flat, round shells reduce the resistance to the water. This habit

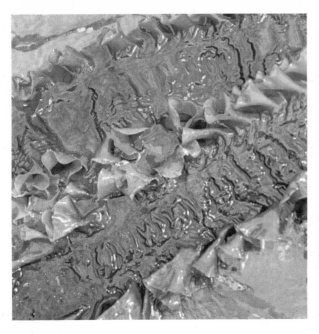

lets them feed on anything brought in by the waves, even the poisonous Portuguese man-o'-war (*Physalia physalia*).

Limpets, of which there are several kinds, are clearly specialists at withstanding the shock of the waves. The conical shell breaks the force of the impact and the grip of the foot prevents the limpet being swept away. Once the limpet has pulled its shell down, it cannot be dislodged without smashing the shell. Quite how the limpet manages this phenomenally hard grip is not known for it is more than simple suction. The shape of the shell varies with degree of exposure, and there is always a clear difference between limpets living on opposite sides of one big boulder. Limpets on the exposed face, or those living high on the shore, have tall shells with a rather narrow base. The shell grows from the base and continual contraction of the muscles

that pull the shell down to avoid wave action or desiccation at high tide, exerts tension on the tissues that secrete the shell and pulls them inwards. On sheltered sites or in rock pools, the shell-secreting tissues are free to spread and the skirt of the shell is broad.

The topography of the shore limits the intensity of wave action. On a steep shore, the waves rear up and break, then pound up the rocks before sliding back with a vicious undertow. A flat shore, perhaps with an almost level platform of rock, takes the brunt of the waves at the lower end so the top will be quite well sheltered. These shores have poor drainage. Water does not drain between waves and upper levels may remain quite wet even at low tide. Species which need frequent wetting can live farther up the shore and there is a progressive shift of normal zonation towards the top of the shore.

Top left: Piddocks are shellfish which bore into the rock with their shells
Bottom left: Sea belt is cast onto the shore after storms. When dry it becomes whitened by a thin crust of sugar crystals, hence its name Laminaria saccharina

Above : Starfish are always depicted as seashore animals but actually live below the tides
Top right : Tangles, an aptly named brown seaweed, are exposed at low spring tide
Bottom right : Purple laver is an edible red seaweed, which forms a slippery film on the rock

The geology of the rocks comprising a shore affects the distribution of sedentary animals and plants by their texture and friability. Barnacles and weeds cannot maintain a hold if the rock is continually crumbling. Sandstone is such a surface and where a vein of hard rock penetrates sandstone, barnacles can be seen on the hard rock while the sandstone is left free for limpets, which may be the sole tenants. Similarly, purple laver replaces the wracks on soft stone.

The softer sandstones, chalks and limestones are the home of the piddock or rock-boring clam (*Pholas dactylus*); the piddock is a bivalve mollusc whose two shells make an auger that drills through rock. Each shell ends in a toothed edge which rasps against the rock as the two shells twist together in a see-saw motion. The piddock grows as it tunnels and so can never escape from its burrow. It must rely for food and respiration on two tubes which protrude from the entrance.

The burrows of piddocks and other borers such as sea urchins, crustaceans, worms and even a species of sponge pepper the soft rockface and provide sheltered places for seaweeds, periwinkles and anemones. This is a good example of one animal modifying the physical environment to benefit other animals. The abrasive action of wrack fronds may prevent barnacle larvae from settling but fields of wracks, like beds of mussels, tend to hold back the drainage of water so that they support populations of small animals that would not otherwise survive so far up the shore. Animals and plants are always competing against, or assisting other members of the community, and relationships mentioned here are reminders that it is pointless to examine any animal or plant separately from the ecological community of which it is an integral part.

Types of Shore

Dividing a shore into zones is only possible because many shore plants and animals are static. Zonation is studied at low tide when periwinkles and limpets are pressed to the rock face, barnacles are closed and other animals are huddled in crevices or buried in sand. This inertia does enable the naturalist to classify the flora and fauna into different levels of the shore, but it also makes behaviour difficult to study.

The Rocky Shore

Along any rocky coast, rockpools are the main centres of activity at low tide, but even there many animals, being nocturnal, lie dormant during the day. In almost all cases, a covering of water is needed to galvanize the inhabitants of a shore into activity. Without it, it is not easy to study behaviour, yet much can be learned even at low tide.

The limpet proves to be a more interesting animal than its stubbornly motionless shell would suggest. A meandering pattern of 'tank tracks' over a rock shows where a limpet has grazed, the tracks being made by the radula, a rasp-like tongue which scrapes up lichens and algae. Two sensory tentacles poke out from under the shell which swings from side to side as the radula browses over the algae. If the rocks remain damp the limpet may even continue feeding at low tide. A limpet may be surrounded by a patch of rock cleared of vegetation which shows the extent of the limpet's movement and, if the rock and limpet are marked with quick-drying paint, a visit at each low tide reveals that the limpet returns to the same spot every day.

On soft sandstone and limestones, the limpet's shell gradually wears a shallow depression into which it fits perfectly. The result is a watertight joint which prevents desiccation at low tide. To fit snugly against hard rock, the edge of the shell has to be moulded. In both cases, the limpet has to return from its wanderings and position itself on the rock so that the shell lines up exactly with the irregularities in the rock. The limpet feeds over a radius of about one metre (3 feet) from its 'home' and it returns by following chemical secretions left on the rock on its outward journey. It also appears to know how far it has travelled on the outward journey and, therefore, how far it has to travel back. When it gets home, it orientates itself by means of a chemical 'template' so that the shell lines up accurately with the rock.

The common European limpet is *Patella vulgata*. Closely related species are to be found the world over, but they are very difficult to tell apart. On Pacific coasts these species are replaced by another limpet, *Acmaea*, one species of which, the tortoiseshell limpet (*Acmaea testudinalis*) is found in Europe. The keyhole limpets (*Diadora* and *Puncturella*) have a slit in the top of the shell through which water circulates, so they cannot stand drying and are found low down on the shore, often under rocks. Related to them are the abalones or ormers. These molluscs are most abundant below the shore but they can be found at the lowest tides, the exception being the black abalone (*Haliotis cracherodii*) which lives in deep crevices of the splash zone. They are greatly prized for their meat and shells and many populations have been severely depleted. Abalones are found in the Mediterranean and in western Europe as far north as the Channel Islands and Brittany. There is an abalone industry in Mexico and California, where there are strict laws conserving the abalones. They may not be collected until 17.5 centimetres (7 inches) long, that is about 12

Left : Few animals or plants could establish themselves on this wave-battered rock surface

years old. To make abalone meat edible it must be pounded with a mallet to break up the fibres. It is then soft and delicious.

Also under the boulders lurks the slipper limpet, which is related more to the periwinkles than the limpets. These animals have a ledge on the inside of the shell which makes the empty shell look rather like a slipper. They live in neat piles of half-a-dozen or so individuals which are permanently stuck together. Grazing off algae, as do limpets or periwinkles, is clearly impossible for such immobile animals and slipper limpets feed like bivalve molluscs by straining minute particles from sea water. Within each chain of slipper limpets, the lowest individuals are female, the highest are male and the middle ones are intermediate in sex. The first limpet to settle automatically becomes female but others that settle on it become male first then turn into females as they grow older. The slipper limpet is American but it was introduced to Britain and has spread across the North Sea. It is a serious pest because it settles on oyster beds, where it competes for food and smothers the oysters.

The chitons or coat-of-mail shells are also armoured molluscs that stick firmly to the underlying rock. Although inconspicuous, they are worth a closer look because they have a row of eight overlapping plates which articulate as the chiton follows the irregular surface of the rock. Most chitons are no more than 1.2 centimetres (0.5 inch) long, but those of Pacific coasts grow much larger. *Cryptochiton stelleri* of the North American west coast grows to 32.5 centimetres (13 inches), with a width of 12.5 centimetres (5 inches). It is called the seaboot or gumboot because it looks like a perished and warped rubber sole when detached from the rock. The chiton has also earned the name sea-cradle because of the curled shape of the detached animal. Most chitons have a life-style similar to that of limpets. They wander over the rocks, grazing algae and probably returning to the same spot, but *Nuttallina californica*, an inhabitant of sheltered shores in California, digs a depression in the rock. Only its back is visible and it feeds on fragments of seaweeds that collect in the depression. It seems that each depression is used by many generations.

The topshells are curious animals, and sometimes mistaken for periwinkles, but they usually show a silvery tip where the shell has been worn. They are as characteristic of rocky shores as periwinkles, more so because periwinkles can live on sand and mud but topshells are confined to rock. They get their name from the resemblance of the conical, spiral shell to a whip-top, once a popular

Above: Rarely seen out of water, an ormer or abalone crawls like a snail over the rocks
Above left: An overturned boulder reveals a keyhole limpet, a cushion star, sponges and limpets sheltering underneath

Above right : Common European limpets clamp to the rock among a crowd of acorn barnacles
Far right : Slipper limpets live in chains, males on top, females underneath

toy. The shell is often prettily coloured and the 10 centimetres (4 inches) diameter *Trochus niloticus* of coral reefs is collected to make pearl buttons. There is a zonation of topshells down the shore, as in periwinkles. Topshells are more susceptible to exposure than periwinkles and most live below the sublittoral fringe, but one European species, *Osilinus lineatus,* lives within a narrow zone at High Water Neaps.

The last of the common rocky shore molluscs, and the most abundant where it occurs, is the mussel. *Mytilus edulis,* the common mussel, lives on both sides of the North Atlantic and around Japan. Other close relatives occur widely; the California mussel (*Mytilus californianus*), the Australian mussel (*Mytilus obscurus*) and the Mediterranean mussel (*Mytilus galloprovincialis*) are so similar to the edible mussel that only experts can tell them apart. The Mediterranean mussel extends north to southern England where it is distinguished from the edible mussel by the darker flesh. The rather different horse mussels live below the shore, except for the American horse mussel (*Modiolus domissus*) which can live for some time out of water. Mussels start as free-living larvae which settle on rock after a month afloat. For a short time they wander over the rock until they have found a suitable place but their

search for space is often as fruitless as any holiday-maker's on a popular beach. As many as 160,000 mussels may crowd, piled one one top of the other, into a square metre.

When it has found a good place to settle, the young mussel anchors itself with tough threads like the guy ropes of a tent, called the byssus. The threads are spun and positioned by the long, extensible foot that protrudes from between the two shells. The byssus threads of the fan mussel (*Pinna fragilis*) are sufficiently strong and long enough to be woven into a cloth which was once valuable because of its golden sheen. Called 'cloth of gold' it was used in garments worn by the aristocracy, particularly of southern Europe. The Field of the Cloth of Gold was a meeting between the Kings of England and France in 1520, and was so named because of the amount of material used by the participants.

The mussel is not completely immobilised by its array of byssus threads. It can pull them in, then put out new threads and cut the old ones, so dragging itself slowly over the rocks. Nevertheless the life-style of mussels is definitely that of a sedentary animal. Reproduction is a simple matter of liberating sperms and eggs into the water, each female laying up to 25 million eggs, and feeding is achieved by straining minute particles out of the

Left : Mediterranean mussels and limpets live among the coralline weeds in a rock pool
Right : This common whelk, its respiratory siphon protruding, carries a sea anemone on its shell

Below : Edible mussel showing growth lines on the shell. It takes several years to attain full size

water in the usual manner of bivalve molluscs. When submerged, the shells gape slightly so that water can be drawn across the gill plates and edible particles trapped on a sheet of mucus. The shells close by two adductor muscles that run between them. If these are cut, the elastic hinge contracts to make the shell open and the fleshy gills can be seen lying pressed together. The workings of the countless cilia whose beating pumps water through the mussel and drives the mucus sheet can be demonstrated by scattering fine powder over the exposed gills.

The limpets, periwinkles, topshells and mussels are the main herbivores of the shore. They are the cattle, if you like, which spend a placid life grazing on algae or filtering bacteria until it is their turn to feed the predators that make up the next level of the food web. The whelks, although relatives of the periwinkles, have become predators on other molluscs and barnacles.

Buccinum undatum, the common whelk, known as the buckie in Scotland and the buccinum in America, lives in the North Atlantic. It was commonly eaten by the Romans and has been fished ever since. The common whelk is not a true shore animal because it is usually found above the low-tide level only as an empty shell or a yellowish mass of egg capsules cast ashore by the waves.

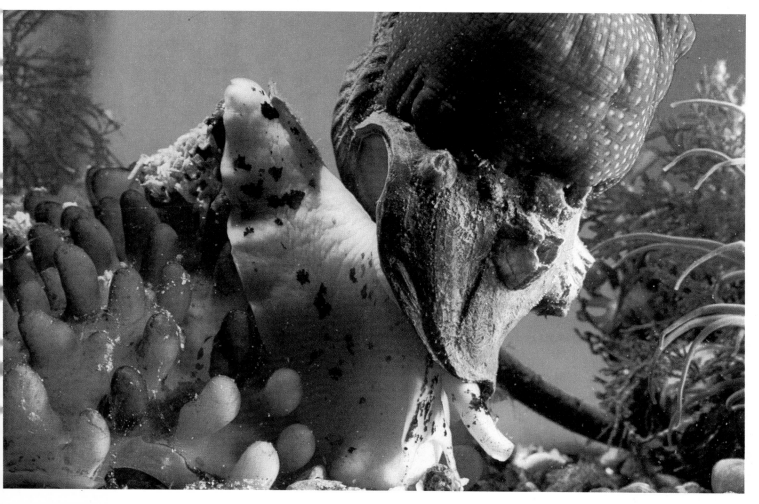

Small whelks can, however, be found at very low tide, particularly where mud and sand have gathered among boulders. Whelks possess an operculum with which to close the opening of the shell, but they do not seem to use it to prevent drying up when caught by a low tide.

Further up the shore there are the smaller dogwhelks (*Nucella*) which can be mistaken for periwinkles until they are lifted from the rock; the mouth of the shell is, however, irregular rather than rounded. At low tide they are often abundant in rock crevices where they huddle among rows of flask-shaped egg capsules that are sometimes mistaken for purse sponges. The shelter of a crevice is particularly needed by dogwhelks living on exposed shores because they do not grip the rocks so firmly as periwinkles or limpets. Nevertheless, they are clearly striving towards survival in rough seas because dogwhelks living in exposed situations have stubby, thick shells. This adaptation allows them to roll about in the surf without harm, while their mouths, which are larger, can maintain a firmer grip with the foot.

Mediterranean whelks, mainly of the genus *Murex*, produce Tyrian purple, the imperial purple of Ancient Rome. The basis of the dye is purpurin, a poison which whelks use to subdue their victims. It starts as a yellow fluid but changes to purple on exposure to sunlight. By the standards of modern synthetic dyes, Tyrian purple is rather dull but it must have been spectacular in its day. The rough whelk tingle or sting winkle (*Ocenebra erinacea*), another lurker under stones, is rather similar to the common whelk. It is important because it attacks oysters, as does *Orosalpinx cinerea*, the oyster drill. The latter is a native of the American east coast which has been accidentally introduced to the west coast of Britain and to Europe. Both also live on mudflats.

The carnivorous habits of whelks are a development of the grazing habit of the periwinkles. The radula, that file-like assembly of teeth which periwinkles use to scrape algae, is modified to pierce the shells and flesh of other animals. The whelk's radula has fewer but larger teeth and is mounted at the tip of a long proboscis. The proboscis is pushed against the prey's flesh and the radula tears a hole so that the tissues can be scooped out. The process is aided by a copious flow of saliva which lubricates and also contains the purpurin to subdue the prey. Common whelks attack open mussels by wedging the edge of the shell between the two shells of the bivalve but dogwhelks bore through the shell of their prey with the radula, probably aided by an acid secretion that dissolves the limy shell. When barnacles

are attacked, the tip of the proboscis is simply forced between the plates of the shell. The diet of any dogwhelk is shown by the colour of its shell. Pale-shelled dogwhelks have eaten barnacles; dark-shelled individuals have eaten mussels. A row of knobs or teeth on the lip of the shell shows that the dogwhelk has suffered a long period on short rations.

The most abundant of the European crabs is the green or shore crab (*Carcinus maenas*). The Pacific shore crabs *Pachygrapsus crassipes* and *Hemigrapsus oregonensis* are in a different family but have rather similar habits. Shore crabs can be found all over the shore, on mudflats, up estuaries and in salt marshes, as well as among rocks, and they are eaten by gulls, oystercatchers and rats, which visit the shores to hunt them, by predatory fishes and even by each other. Despite the hostile attentions of so many different creatures, they defend themselves bravely – the French call them *le crabe enragé* because they threaten with their claws raised. If you can brave their fierce appearance, they repay close attention. A shore crab can be recognised by the five notches or teeth on the edge of the shell. Tucked under its body, is the 'tail', the equivalent of the long abdomen of the lobster. Female crabs have a broad, seven-jointed tail; that of the male is narrow and five-

jointed. Sometimes the larger male can be found clasping the female, ready to mate with her. Or the female will be 'in berry', carrying an orange, rough mass of eggs on her tail. Alternatively, there may be a smooth, doughy, lemon- or orange-coloured, mass bulging under the tail. This is the reproductive part of a parasitic barnacle *Sacculina*. *Sacculina* starts life as a larva, like any other barnacle, but it settles on the body of a crab and penetrates its body. Gradually it sends slender growths like roots throughout the crab's body and absorbs nutrients from the crab's body fluids. The crab survives but it can neither breed nor shed its shell at intervals as would a normal crab. Furthermore, male crabs are turned into hermaphrodites by this parasite. They assume the tail configuration of females but cannot lay eggs.

When the parasitizing *Sacculina* dies, the crab is free to moult again. All arthropods, or joint-legged animals, which include insects, spiders and scorpions as well as crabs, shrimps and other crustaceans, have external, rigid skeletons which must be shed and replaced to allow the animal to grow. Molluscs do not have this constraint because their shells grow continuously. Before the moult is due, the crab reabsorbs much of the material of the shell back into its body, in the

Above: The rough whelk tingle lives on both rocky and mud shores
Above left: Dogwhelks huddle in a rock crevice at low tide
Above right: The European shore crab is recognized by the teeth on the edge of its shell
Right: Female velvet swimming crab carrying a mass of eggs under her abdomen

interests of economy. At the same time it grows a new shell underneath. Then, the crab absorbs large amounts of water and its body swells. The old now brittle shell falls off and the new shell, which is flexible, expands. Meanwhile the crab hides under a stone while its new shell hardens.

Many shore crabs will be found to have one or more legs missing, a sign that the crab has fallen foul either of a predator or of boulders tumbling in the swell. The crab meets these threats by effortlessly shedding the trapped limb. There is a special brittle 'breaking plane' near the base of the limb and the contraction of a muscle twists the limb to snap it across the plane. The exposed wound is protected by a membrane except where a blood vessel and the nerves run and this gap is soon sealed by a blood clot. A new limb starts to grow immediately and is complete after three months.

Shore crabs are scavengers and predators. They eat anything living or dead that they can deal with, trying anything. A schoolboy pastime is catching shore crabs by danging a pebble, suspended from a line, in front of them. The pebble is seized in the claws and the crab is whipped out before it realizes that it has made a bad choice.

Near the bottom of the shore the small edible crabs (*Cancer pagurus*) may be found. There will also be the velvet fiddler crab (*Portunus puber*) which is a swimming crab with broad, paddle-shaped rear limbs and a velvety pile of hairs over its body. The pea crab (*Pinnotheres*) will not be found without a special exploration. The female lives in mussels where she uses her bristly claws to steal food from the mussel's gills. The smaller male creeps into the mussels to mate with her. Other species of pea crab live in sea urchins, sea cucumbers and sea squirts.

The porcelain crabs are somewhat different from the other crabs because their abdomens are asymmetrical. They feed by straining particles out of the water with bristly mouthparts and survive on exposed shores where their flattened bodies allow them to hide under stones and in crevices. They too throw off their limbs very easily, which may also be an adaptation for survival under the force of the surf.

The asymmetrical abdomen links the porcelain crabs with the hermit crabs. The hermit crabs give themselves away when a shell of periwinkle, topshell or whelk scuttles across the floor of a pool at a speed unbelievable for a mollusc. This speeding shell has been taken over by the crab which has no shell of its own, and the asymmetric abdomen, which does not curl forwards as in other crabs, fills the coils of the shell. The hermit crab

Above : Red crabs scuttle over the shore in search of anything edible, including parasites on the skins of marine iguanas
Above right : The pea crab lives within the shell of an edible mussel
Right : Hermit crabs often protect themselves with the abandoned shells of shellfish

is held in place by some of the legs and hooked appendages at the tip of the abdomen and, when danger threatens, the crab retreats into the shell and seals the opening with one claw, which is larger than the other. Some odd alternatives to mollusc shells are the use of bamboo stems and coconut shells by *Coenobita* crabs. *Coenobita diogenes* of Bermuda uses the shell of the now extinct snail *Livona pica*.

As the hermit crab grows it needs to move to larger shells. In fact, there used to be a dwarf race of the Mediterranean hermit crab (*Clibanarius*) living in the Black Sea. Its stunted growth was due to the lack of large molluscs in the Black Sea but since the large Japanese snail *Rapana* was accidentally introduced in 1947, the crabs have grown to take full advantage of the more roomy accommodation. Changing from one shell to another is a traumatic event for the hermit

crab, as it is vulnerable during the manoeuvre. It searches for a suitable empty shell and tests it very carefully with its claws. When satisfied, it gets into position and slips from one shell to the other as if embarrassed to show its naked abdomen.

The feeding habits of the hermit crab are a combination of the scavenging of the shore crab and the filter-feeding of the porcelain crab. Added to the lure of their solid home, this attracts a number of hangers-on. There is a ragworm *Nereis fucata* which hides in the shell and reaches out to steal scraps of food. Some hermit crabs carry sponges which also feed on scraps, as does the delicate pink hydroid, a distant relative of the anemones, that grows on European hermit crabs.

The most interesting example of mutual 'back-scratching' exists between hermit crabs and sea

Above: Sea anemones survive by withdrawing their tentacles and closing their mouths at low tide. Lining up below them is a chiton Right: Sea cucumbers have the strange habit of ejecting thin streamers when disturbed

anemones, which take advantage of the hermit crab as a mobile base and bend over to sweep up particles of food. In return, the anemone's stinging cells protect the crab from octopuses and other predators. The common European hermit crab (*Pagurus bernhardus*) will carry one or more of the anemone *Calliactis parasitica*. When the crab changes shells it transfers the anemones with its claws, but *Pagurus prideauxi* carries *Adamsia palliata* which forms a cloak over the crab. The crab does not change shells but, as it grows, the anemone expands to cover it. The crab *Paguropsis typica* dispenses with a shell altogether and relies wholly on its anemone for protection.

The molluscs and crabs are the most obvious members of the rocky shore, and to most visitors to the shore, they are the most interesting. Other animals are usually overlooked and ignored, if only because they hide under boulders or among dense mats of seaweed. They are often inconspicuous, inactive and not very attractive. They include worms of various kinds and strange creatures from far-flung, unfamiliar corners of the animal kingdom.

Two of the more common lesser animals are the tube-worms *Spirorbis* and *Pomatoceros*. *Spirorbis* lives in a small, coiled chalky tube attached to the frond of a wrack and looks more like a snail than a worm. *Pomatoceros* has a long, wriggling tube, attached to rocks. It has a ridge along the top and a spine over the mouth. Low on the shores of the warmer parts of the American Pacific seaboard, there is a mollusc that can easily be mistaken for a tube-worm. Known only by the scientific name *Aletes squamosus*, this snail lives under boulders and has given up moving in search of food. Instead of grazing like a periwinkle, it captures floating food particles in a net of mucus. As it grows, the snail builds a chalky tube from the mouth of its shell very much like a worm tube.

Also found on wrack fronds and rocks are encrustations of sea mats or polyzoans. These are colonies of small animals that look rather like a small piece of lace and are easily mistaken for plants, or perhaps a sponge. There are colonies of sea squirts whose bodies are encased in a gelatinous case or tunic. Like the sponges and bivalve molluscs such as the mussel, the sea squirts feed by drawing a current of water through the body and straining off minute, edible particles. They get their name from the two spurts of water that jet from the inlet and outlet apertures when the sea squirt is prodded. Some sea squirts are solitary, others live in colonies. The colonial habit is common among these small, sedentary animals. Another group is the hydroids, relatives of the anemones and jellyfish. Each has a skeleton which supports the delicate tissues and looks like a delicate, leafless tree. The common name of one of these hydroids – the sea oak (*Dynamena pumila*) – reflects this curious similarity.

The protection of the wracks and boulders allows some of the animals of the sublittoral zone to penetrate the sublittoral fringe where they can be found at the lowest spring tides. Among them are the brittlestars, slender-armed relatives of the starfish. Some catch microscopic food on a net of mucus; others are herbivores, feeding on seaweeds, and a third group eats worms and crustaceans. A few species of starfish can be found here, as well as two other members of the major animal group Echinodermata.

Animals of this group have bodies built on a plan of five radiating arms. The plan is obvious in the starfish and brittlestars but can also be seen in

Overleaf: The velvet swimming crab or velvet fiddler crab shows the flat, paddle-shaped rear legs that distinguish it as a good swimmer. It is commonly found among weeds and stones at low tide

the spherical sea-urchins and tubular sea cucumbers. Sea-urchin shells, known as tests, are popular as ornaments and the gonads, or sex organs, of sea urchins are eaten. Those of the 16 centimetres (6 inches) long sea-urchin *Stronglyocentrus* are eaten by Italians, both on their native shores and where people of Italian origin have settled in California. The big sea cucumber *Stichopus* of the Pacific, known as the *bêche de mer* and considered by the Chinese to be an aphrodisiac, is eaten after being boiled and dried. Sea cucumbers have the bizarre habit of eviscerating themselves when disturbed, and the small western European *Cucumarea* species are called cotton-spinners because they exude a mass of mucus threads that trap any predator attempting to prise them from the safety of rock clefts.

The Tide's Edge

One of the main problems for seashore animals is drying up. Normally, there is a period of about twelve hours between high tide and low tide, so that a typical seashore animal has to adjust from a wholly aquatic environment to a terrestrial environment twice a day – the greatest possible change for a living organism. It would be a mistake, however, to suppose that many shore animals spend half their time exposed to the drying effects of air and half to immersion in water.

The simple fact of living between the two elements is paramount in determining the ecology of shore animals. For example, the area between the high-tide mark and mid-tide level is comparatively barren of animal life, except for organisms such as the limpets, barnacles and some periwinkles, which can shut themselves off from the air and are therefore capable of surviving unusually long periods of desiccation. It is at low-tide mark that the shore begins to be populated with a great variety of species. On a typical beach there may be only half a dozen species of animals to be found above mid-tide level, as compared with the dozens of animals to be found nearer the sea. The experienced shore-collector therefore postpones his activities until three hours after high tide.

Most shore animals spend not more than three hours out of every twelve exposed to the drying effects of wind and sun. Many spend much less time than this because they normally live nearer the low-tide mark. Even so, this relatively short period of twice-daily exposure would be lethal if these species did not have some way of keeping moist or of retaining water for respiration. There are several ways in which this can be accomplished. One of the least obvious is found in sponges.

To most people a sponge is something to use in the bath. However, bath sponges represent only a handful of sponge species and these generally grow below the low-tide mark and in the warmer tropical and subtropical waters of the world. The remaining two and a half thousand species not only have no commercial value but are known only to naturalists.

The sponges living on the shore are usually shapeless encrustations on rocks and seaweeds, often brightly coloured, usually in red, orange or yellow, recognizable by their crater-like vents. They are very numerous on rocky shores, covering the rock surfaces in much the same manner as lichens cover the rocks on land. They also, like lichens, appear to be fully exposed to the drying effects of the elements at low tide. Indeed, scientists have long speculated on how sponges with their delicate tissues and great need of water

Above: Huge numbers of cockleshells thrown up after a storm in the Dutch Wadden Zee

Top: Sea slugs are shellfish which do not have shells. They are often beautifully coloured

Bottom: Sponges can often be found in pools and squeezed into rock crevices where they precariously survive low tide

spied on for the whole low-tide period. Close observation will reveal that the sponge is growing in a depression in the rock so slight as to be almost unnoticeable at a casual glance. Yet the rim of the depression is such that, as the sun travels across the sky, the sponge, a low encrustation only a few millimetres thick, is always in the shade, or partial shade, cast by the rim of the depression.

Another clue to survival lies in the labyrinth of tiny canals which traverse the body of a sponge. These retain enough water for the sponge's reduced respiration. A hibernating land mammal may only breathe some five times a minute compared with, say, 200 times a minute during normal activity. This rate of breathing is just high enough to keep the life processes ticking over until the animal awakes and resumes normal activity. While they are uncovered, many seashore animals go into a state of suspended animation resembling hibernation. They retain only sufficient water within the body to keep their metabolism going at a very low ebb. This is true for sea anemones, sea squirts, moss animals and others that close up when the tide falls. Such animals site themselves so as to make the maximum use of shade or semi-shade. So the subtle adaptations of the sponges are not exclusive ruses to retain life-giving moisture, they are typical of many shore animals.

Sponges point the way to survival under the seemingly harsh conditions of the seashore in another way. They share with a very few animal groups a capacity for 100 per cent regeneration. It is possible to take a lump of living sponge, place it in a fine cloth such as silk, squeeze it and separate its component cells, which pass through the meshes of the silk as a milky liquid. If this liquid is allowed to fall into a glass dish of sea water and viewed under a microscope the separate cells can be seen slithering about, amoeba-like, on the bottom of the dish. Slowly, taking hours in the process, the cells meet up and join in groups. These groups continue to move about and they also coalesce until several small functional sponges are formed. These, partly by moving, partly by growing larger and so reaching out to each other, could in time reform into a perfect sponge the size of the original lump.

It can happen, although it is rare on temperate shores, that an encrusting sponge grows where it can become almost dried up during a period of low tide and hot weather. In such a case those cells not killed by the sun's heat become amoeboid. They wander through the meshes of the skeleton, coalesce and form groups, and eventually regenerate to form roughly the sponge as it originally existed. No doubt if the summer sun was protracted, the sponge might eventually die off, but

are able to withstand the dire effects of twice-daily exposure. No satisfactory explanation was found until the experts realized that sponges avoid desiccation rather than endure it.

The position of sponges on the shore partly explains their survival. They do not live higher than mid-tide level, unless they are in a large rock pool which is permanently full. Below mid-tide level they are most numerous on the under-surfaces of overhanging rocks or on those surfaces protected by curtains of seaweed. Best of all, and most abundantly, they grow in caves or cave-like situations, such as the cavities within piles of boulders, where the walls remain damp and the atmosphere is very humid.

There are some sponges that grow on the vertical surfaces of rocks, apparently exposed to the full glare of the sun, yet never dry out. This seeming paradox is only resolved if the animal is

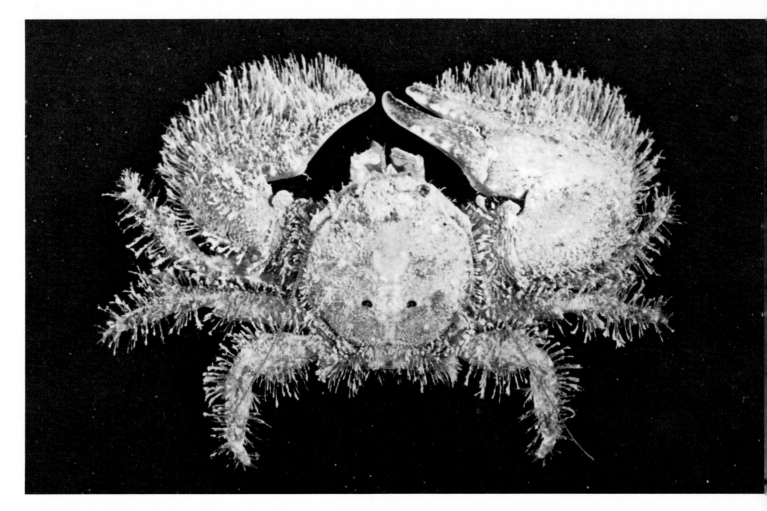

with this remarkable regenerative capacity it has a reasonable chance of surviving even a long spell of hot days.

This power of wholesale regeneration is found only in aquatic invertebrates without an external skeleton, and mainly in those whose members are represented on the seashore. They include sea squirts and sea anemones. Some sea anemones reproduce by leaving pieces of their base on the rocks as they move about, each piece growing into a new anemone, others split into two to produce two complete anemones by regeneration of the torn surfaces.

A good power of regeneration aids survival from predation. Sponges and sea anemones cannot escape predators so it is useful to be able to heal the gaping wounds caused by sea slugs, for instance. Sea slugs are shell-less molluscs and are the most brightly coloured animals of the seashore. The sea lemon (*Archidoris pseudoargus*) is a large, common sea slug. It is yellow mottled with red and green and is one of the few shore animals to feed on sponges.

The habits of the sponge point a general lesson about shore animals. Sponges are capable of movement from place to place only when young and then very slowly and to a limited extent. Thus the place where the larvae settle decides their fate;

if rigorously unfavourable, they are soon killed off by exposure. Regeneration helps survival only against intermittently adverse conditions. Crabs and fishes living on the shore can move about and choose safe places by their superior powers of locomotion. The same search for damp and shade governs where they go. Crabs, lobsters, even sea urchins and starfishes, can, on a falling tide, burrow into sand, hide under rocks or stones, shelter under the hanging curtains of seaweed, take advantage of shade, and, to some extent, go into a partial state of suspended activity. They can also seek out rock pools, as the most inexperienced seashore collector soon discovers. Rock pools yield the highest density of shore animals, and may even hold an octopus that has strayed up from the depths. It is a rewarding occupation to lift the seaweed curtains and to search under rocks and boulders for animals taking shelter while the tide is out. This is where the flat-bodied animals such as the porcelain crabs and the flat encrustations of sponges enjoy an advantage, as they take shelter in the narrow space beneath a slab or rock lying on the shore. A whole community of half a dozen kinds of animals may be found under a slab of rock the size of a dinner plate.

This community may include small fishes, for a minority of the animals left behind by the receding

Above : The broad-clawed porcelain crab is a relative of the hermit crabs. It lives under stones on muddy shores

tide are fishes, especially gobies. They, like the crabs, are fully mobile and can choose where they go. The means by which they survive exposure include their scales, an outer skeleton which is almost impervious to water.

The tiny amount of water needed for a fish to survive is well illustrated by the case of the fish and the postman. A flatfish had been caught at sea and was to be dispatched to a Scottish fisheries laboratory for investigation. Since it was immaterial to the scientists whether the fish arrived dead or alive, it was dropped into a small plastic bag, placed in a box and sent through the post. It arrived at its destination the following day, still alive and seemingly none the worse for having been out of water apart from the very small amount clinging to its body when dropped into the bag. The restricted space kept the fish quiescent and the dampness inside the bag was sufficient, presumably, for its respiratory needs.

Shore fishes can find themselves in situations similar to that of the flatfish in the post. Normally they keep to the rock pools, beautifully camouflaged and hidden, sheltering among the small seaweeds and corallines or under an overhang of rock at the edge of the pool. When disturbed they dart, with a rapid serpentine wriggling of the body, across the pool into another hide-out. Their actions show that, like the various species on land, they retain a memory of their various bolt-holes and can move unerringly to them at a moment's notice. It has recently been discovered that at least one kind of shore goby can leap from one rock pool to another with great accuracy, even when the second pool is hidden from its sight by an intervening rock. The assumption is that fishes have the same remarkable knowledge of the physical features of the environment that has excited wonder in the case of birds and mammals. Such a propensity is even more remarkable in fishes, with their lower mental equipment.

Some seashore fishes seem almost to scorn the use of rock pools, relying on wet curtains of seaweeds or dripping rock overhangs. When disturbed they slither along damp gulleys in a rocky substratum or over layers of seaweed.

Some gobies rely on animal neighbours for safety. Those of the genus *Smilogobius*, of the Indo-Pacific, share a burrow with a snapping shrimp. The goby stays nearby while the shrimp excavates the burrow. When danger threatens the goby dives into the burrow, followed by the shrimp. Once the alarm has subsided the fish emerges, followed by the shrimp, which seems to have complete confidence in the goby's acute senses.

Below : The rocky goby is a solitary species living in rock pools. The pelvic fins form a sucker to grip the rock

On the coast of California lives a blind goby *Typhlogobius californiensis*, which also shares a shrimp's burrow but, once inside, remains there. Some small gobies live in sponges. Their presence in these is not accidental, since they are covered in only a few rows of long, spiny scales. These are used as climbing irons by which the fish moves up and down the smooth inner surfaces of the canals spreading throughout the sponge body.

Shore fishes can even hold their breath, that is, make use of water contained in their gill cavities while not immersed. This is taken to an extreme in the mudskippers of mangrove swamps. These leave the sea and hop or skip over the mud. While out of water they rely on water in the gill chambers and on having the skin lining of the mouth and throat rich in blood vessels so that it acts as a secondary gill. At fairly frequent intervals the mudskipper must go to a pool on the shore to replenish its water supply. In doing this the fish, of course, dips its head into the water. Often, as it turns to go away, its tail also momentarily dips into the water. This beguiled some observers into believing that it breathed through its tail.

Sandy and Muddy Shores
As the tide goes out, the flat expanse of a sandy or muddy shore looks disappointing to the naturalist.

A sandy beach appears fit only for building sand-castles and a mudflat seems to offer no possibilities at all. However, the birds feeding along the tide's edge will confirm that the shore cannot be completely bare of marine life. A closer inspection will show definite signs of occupation: small tunnels leading into the sand, wormcasts, and empty shells washed up after a storm. In fact, a sandy or muddy shore is swarming with life, and there may be a greater mass of animal life on these unpromising expanses than on the richest rocky shore. It is simply that the animals are out of sight, living a troglodyte existence underground, at least while the tide is out. Because the world of these shores is hidden, much less is known about the lives of their inhabitants than of those on a rocky shore. Even to collect the animals requires considerable physical fitness because large amounts of sand or mud must be dug up and sieved to separate out the inhabitants.

There is no fixed boundary between sandy and muddy shores. Sand consists of coarse particles and mud is composed of fine particles and there are various gradations of muddy sand and sandy mud. On a single stretch of coastline, a shingle beach of large, rounded pebbles can grade into a sandy beach and thence into a mudflat. Each stage of the series has its own physical characteristics

Below: A sandy beach can be a rich source of food. These balls of sand have been cleared of nutrients by fiddler crabs

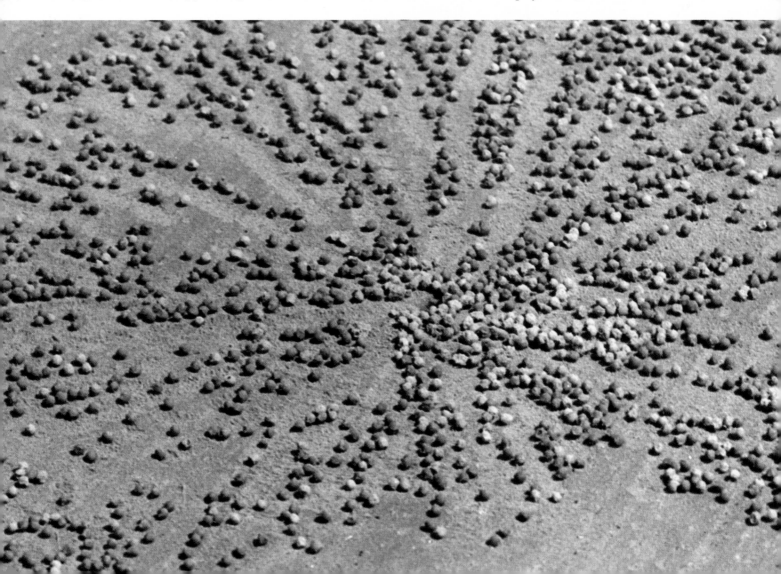

on which depend the type of animal life that can
live in it.

Shingle beaches are formed where there is
maximum exposure to wave action. The force of
the wave piles the pebbles into a steep bank which
drains freely between each wave and grinds the
pebbles together, so wearing them smooth. Little
or no plant or animal life can survive this continual pounding and the undertow between incoming waves sucks out any finer particles.
Shingle beaches are found at the top of the shore
and they culminate in storm beaches which are
ramparts of loaf-sized boulders thrown up into
the splash zone by the heaviest storms.

Below the shingle beach, or on sheltered shores
where wave action is slighter, sandy beaches form
from small particles of rock and shells. The slope is
more gradual and the beach more stable. Sand
holds water; each grain is covered with a film of
moisture that acts as a lubricant to prevent
abrasion. As the beach levels out and becomes
more sheltered, organic material in the form of
animal and plant remains accumulates until
inorganic material is in the minority and the
result is mud. The inorganic material is usually
silt or clay which can become so compacted that
the mudflat is a hard pavement, almost rock-like,
rather than sludge.

Both sand and mud hold water well at low tide
so they can be colonized by marine animals but,
on organically rich beaches, oxygen in the contained water is rapidly used up. The boundary
between oxygenated and de-oxygenated conditions
is often shown by a black layer, sometimes offen-
sive with hydrogen sulphide (rotten egg gas). It lies
from a few millimetres down in mud to several
metres down in clean sand. The water content has
another important influence on animal life in that
it affects the hardness of the sand or mud. Some
kinds of sand dry out easily, becoming hard-
packed under pressure and consequently difficult
for burrowing animals to penetrate. Other kinds
of sand are very wet and pressure from a human
foot or a burrowing animal causes them to become
boggy. Quicksands become liquid under pressure
and swallow up the unwary.

The range of sandy and muddy shores houses
a variety of animal communities but there is less
variety here than on a rocky shore. Bivalve
molluscs and annelid worms dominate in numbers
of both species and individuals. In the Wadden
Zee of Holland, for instance, a density of 2000
cockles per square metre has been recorded.
Although superficially a barren desert, this kind
of shore is an equable, rich environment.

Very little lives at the surface except for shrimps,

63

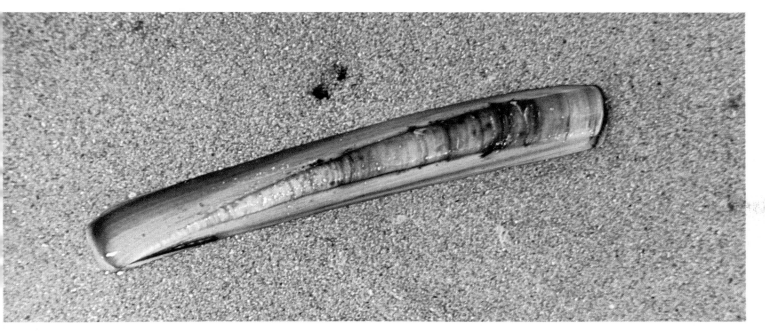

the laver spire shell (*Hydrobia ulvae*), and the ghost and fiddler crabs of tropical beaches. *Hydrobia* frequents muddy shores in vast numbers. As the tide comes in, it surfaces and is carried up the shore. It secretes a raft of mucus to help it float and to trap edible particles. On the tide's retreat, the snail crawls over the mud in search of food, then buries itself to continue feeding underground. Shrimps stay buried while the tide is out and come up to feed only when the water covers them. They can be caught by driving a net through shallow water.

By burrowing under the surface, animals are saved some of the problems facing those on a rocky shore. Unless the beach is being eroded, they are safe from wave action and the blanket of sand or mud protects them from extremes of temperature. The heat of a tropical sun does not penetrate more than a few centimetres and a cold spell in winter may leave a layer of ice covering the beach but the frost does not penetrate. Moreover, there is no danger of desiccation as water does not drain away as the tide drops; a hole dug in the sand soon fills with water.

The problem that these animals do face is how to move through the resisting, smothering mass of sand. In general, animals living under the surface do not travel far during a lifetime, but many move short distances in search of food and must be able to sink themselves into the sand or mud if exposed by tidal action. The two common groups of beach animals, the bivalves and the worms, employ the same method of burrowing. Being soft-bodied, they have to force their way through the sand where a hard-bodied animal with limbs, such as a shrimp or a crab, can burrow by digging with its legs.

The soft-bodied animal uses its blood pressure to change the shape of its body and alternately pulls and pushes its way through the sand. First it expands its body to brace itself, then it probes forward with the head, in the case of worms, or foot, as in bivalves. The 'probe' is kept slender to facilitate burrowing and, when fully extended, the tip is distended to make an anchor, thereby locking the front of the animal in place. Blood pressure is then reduced in the body so that it can release its grip and muscular contraction draws it forward, towards the anchored front end. Movement of a bivalve's body is aided by a squirt of water from between the shells to loosen the sand ahead of it.

Naturally, a slender shape makes movement easier and animals living in coarse-grained sand are streamlined. The well-named razorshells, or jack-knife clams in America, are typical of clean, sandy beaches where they live near the low-tide mark. They lie vertically in the sand with the long foot protruding downwards. While the tide is in, the razorshells lie just below the surface but sink deeper when exposed. There is little to reveal their presence except perhaps a slight depression in the beach from which a jet of water may erupt. An incautious approach makes the razorshells sink deeper, their slim bodies allowing a very rapid retreat when vibrations in the sand warn of approaching danger. Razorshells were eaten at one time and mythology tells that they were served at the wedding of Hebe, daughter of Zeus. Neapolitan fishermen used to catch razorshells by steadying themselves on a staff, then feeling for the shell with the naked foot. Once located, the shell was grasped between the toes, a technique that often resulted in deep cuts. A simpler method is to drop a pinch of salt in the razorshell's burrow. The irritation drives it to the surface.

The wedge shells (*Donax*) are slender, prettily

65

coloured bivalves that live in hard, clean sands. They are quite remarkable animals because they travel up and down the shore with the tide. As the tide begins to rise the shells are buried in the sand, then, as a heavy wave crashes over them, they leap out and are carried up in the swash, burying themselves before the water drains away. In this way they move higher and higher up the shore until the tide starts to ebb, when they reverse the process.

By contrast with the slim razorshells and the narrow wedge shells, cockles and gapers (the soft-shelled clams of America) are stout and progress through the sand only slowly as the blunt shell is worked to and fro in a digging motion. As a gaper grows, its foot becomes relatively smaller and the adult clam is barely able to move. The largest mud-dweller is the geoduck (pronounced go-ee-duck) of the western United States which grows to 6 kilogrammes (13 pounds) and lives 2 metres (6.5 feet) deep.

When a razorshell or cockle moves through sand, the grains flow in behind to conceal signs of the animal's passage, but many beach-dwellers construct burrows which remain open to allow a flow of water to bathe the occupant. On exposed sandy beaches, wave action destroys fragile structures so the tube-building worms are most common in sheltered parts of the beach. Even so, a storm leaves the beach littered with the tubes of the worm *Pectinaria*. Each tube is 3–4 centimetres (1–1.5 inches) long and is made of carefully-graded sand grains which are glued with mucus so precisely that they fit together face-to-face. *Pectinaria* carries its tube with it, rather as a caddis larva carries its case around the bottom of a pond. It lives head downwards in the sand with the tip of the tube just protruding above the surface while it burrows by means of tentacles. The sand mason is another tube-worm that constructs a neat home of cemented sand. The sand mason's tube is permanently fixed. It may be up to 25 centimetres (10 inches) long and the worm retreats to the bottom at low tide. Muddy shores may be covered with the projecting tubes of the lovely peacock worm (*Sabella pavonina*). When covered by the tide the peacock worm unfolds a ring of coloured tentacles which trap food particles from the water.

Burrowing animals have two major sources of food. They can find sustenance among the sand and mud particles or they can extract it from the water above. The differences between the two sources are far-reaching and result in two basic ecological divisions among the mud and sand burrowers. Taking food from the sand or mud is called deposit feeding and deposit feeders are

most likely to be found on muddy beaches. Here the inorganic silt is mixed with organic matter, such as fragments of seaweed, and the fine particles provide a large surface area for the growth of bacteria.

Extracting food from water is known as filter feeding. The animal inhales a stream of water and passes it over some form of sieve where edible particles, such as minute planktonic plants and animals, are strained off. At the same time, oxygen is extracted from the water for respiration.

The lugworm or lobworm, *Arenicola marina*, is a non-selective deposit feeder that eats everything in front of it. Anything organic, from bacteria to animal remains, is digested and the inorganic remainder is voided to the surface as the familiar wormcast. The lugworm's feeding habits are very similar to those of its relative the earthworm but the latter is continually boring through the soil

Top: Tellins are usually found buried in sand with only their tubular siphons protruding above the surface
Bottom: Wedge shells are remarkably agile shellfish which move up and down the shore with the tide

66

Top: A lugworm about to burrow into the sand. It eats sand, digesting edible fragments, and ejecting grains as a cast Bottom: The beautiful peacock worm lives in a tube and catches minute food particles in its fan of tentacles

eater. It lives 15–20 centimetres (6–8 inches) under the surface of sandy beaches in large numbers but is usually seen only as a fragile, heart-shaped shell cast up after a storm. The dense covering of spines which it uses for tunnelling through the sand has usually disappeared by this stage. Unlike the lugworm which has its food brought to it, the heart urchin must move continuously, drawing sand grains to its mouth where edible organic material is scraped off and swallowed. Along with the sand the heart urchin also scoops up baby mussels and other newly settled animals which greatly enrich its coarse diet. To breathe, the urchin maintains a flue to the surface through which a stream of water is drawn. As it moves forwards, the long tube-feet that held the flue open are withdrawn and a new flue is constructed about two body-lengths along the direction of travel.

The amount of sand that these animals must process to make a living is shown by the ragworm *Thoracophelia mucronata* of California. Each worm scoops up and swallows 21 kilogrammes (46 pounds) of sand per year, of which one per cent is digestible organic matter. Over 3,000 of these worms will inhabit each square metre of shore.

Other deposit feeders comb the surface for diatoms and organic detritus. The tellins, or sunset shells, and wedge shells are bivalve molluscs with delicately coloured, slender shells. They live just below the surface and scour the surrounding water with a long tubular siphon. The siphon acts like a vacuum cleaner, sucking up water and fine particles. The particles are strained off into the mouth and the water is ejected through a short exhalant siphon. The inhalant siphon is not long enough to draw in sufficient food, although movements of the sea are continually bringing fresh supplies. However, these molluscs can easily move to new feeding grounds because their slender shells allow them to progress quite rapidly through the sand. Another common deposit feeder is the furrow shell (*Scrobicularia*) which lives 15 centimetres (6 inches) deep in the soft mud of estuaries.

The tellins also take advantage of the other source of food. They are filter feeders as well as deposit feeders, the change in habit being easily effected by raising the siphons above the surface so that they can draw in large quantities of sea water. Animals that specialize in filter feeding characteristically have the inhalant and exhalant siphons joined together except at the tips. They are less mobile and just protrude beyond the surface. As familiar examples of filter feeders we have the cockle, razorshell, gaper and Venus shell species.

while the lugworm remains stationary in its U-shaped burrow.

The tail shaft of the burrow is lined with mucus to keep its walls solid and the worm backs up to avoid its cast. The head shaft is filled with a column of sand and the worm continually swallows sand at the base. This sand is replaced by the column slipping down, which results in the familiar depression in the beach surface. At each high tide, the swirling water refills the shaft with fresh sand so that the worm has a continuous supply of food brought to it. While sand is moving through the burrow from head to tail, movements of the worm's body pump water from tail to head for respiratory purposes. Small planktonic organisms are trapped in the sand in front of the worm's mouth and add to organic material swallowed by the worm.

The heart urchin is another underground sand

The pumping mechanism that draws the stream of water through the siphons of bivalve molluscs consists of myriads of cilia. These are microscopic 'hairs' that cover the animal's gills and maintain a continuous rhythmic beating. The flow of water provides oxygen for respiration and particles are strained from it by a fine sheet of mucus that flows over the gills and is impelled towards the mouth by the cilia. Only fine particles are retained in the mucus and larger particles are thrown out, so that the gills are working rather like a mechanical grader. They do not distinguish between edible and inedible particles; the separation is only by size. However, diatoms, dinoflagellates and bacteria fall within the size limits selected by the mucus grader and the final separation of edible material takes place in the stomach.

A noteworthy feature of animals that spend their lives buried under the beach is the simplicity of their senses. The bivalve molluscs cannot be said even to have heads and their nervous systems are very simple. Not surprisingly, eyes are not well developed in these burrowing animals but the bivalves have simple light-sensitive organs at the tips of the siphons so they can detect the approaching shadow of a predator and quickly retract beneath the surface. Many burrowing animals are also extremely sensitive to vibrations; the razorshell, for instance, retreats downwards very rapidly when it detects approaching footsteps.

The reduced sense organs are a function of life in a uniform environment in which the animals do not need elaborate behaviour to seek food or shelter. Shelter is provided by the sand or mud that they live in and food is all about them in abundance. Their senses are mainly concerned with sorting edible from inedible particles and

detecting the approach of danger.

These burrowers are actually not so secure from danger as they might seem. Although safe from the waves' action, their huge numbers attract a wide variety of predators. Apart from the birds which probe and dig along the shore, there are a number of predatory burrowers which follow the deposit and filter feeders into their own world. The ragworm, a more active cousin of the lugworm and earthworm, tunnels actively in search of prey. Each ring or segment of the body bears a pair of paddle-shaped limbs with which the worm swims or crawls. The head is armed with a pair of jaws carried on a proboscis that is everted and shot out to seize prey. The catworm or white cat, *Nephthys hombergi*, is a ragworm with a mother-of-pearl sheen and its close relative, known only by the scientific name of *Glycera* is yellowish and has the habit of coiling up when disturbed. Both live in sand and are replaced in estuarine mudflats by the common ragworm (*Nereis diversicolor*), recognizable by the red line running down its back. These carnivorous worms are opportunists, they eat any live or dead animals that they can manage.

One prize to be found in sand or mud is the sea mouse whose corpse is occasionally found lying on the surface. This is a most deceptive animal. At first sight it looks like a 15 centimetres (6 inches) long, bristly slug. When the sand or mud is washed off, the sea mouse shows its true colours as bristles are revealed in iridescent metallic colours that change from gold or red and scarlet to lilac or yellow and orange, according to how the light strikes them. This is why the sea mouse is called *Aphrodite*, after the Greek goddess of beauty. The bristles run in two rows down the flanks and the back is covered with a mat of fine

Above : The ragworm is an active predator which pursues slow-moving animals

68

hairs. When turned on its back, the sea mouse displays some familiar features. It is a scale worm related to the ragworms and the underside of the body is divided into segments like a concertina, each segment bearing a pair of paddle-like limbs tipped with stout bristles. It lives just below the surface of the sand, with its hind end protruding. Under the mat of hairs on its back is a double row of overlapping plate-like scales, which form a roof over the body. A stream of water for respiratory purposes is drawn in by the hind end and circulates around the body before being passed back under the scales. Very little is known of the sea mouse's life except that it feeds on carrion and other worms that are too slow to escape from it. A Caribbean relative, the fireworm (*Odontosyllis enopla*) lives on coral reefs and uses its fine bristles as a defence. Merely brushing against the fireworm snaps the bristles which penetrate the skin like slivers of glass and set up a burning irritation that is made worse by rubbing.

Another good find is a sand dollar or cake urchin. This is a flattened, disc-shaped sea urchin which lives on the sand surface or just beneath. Sand dollars are most abundant in the warmer American and Japanese waters. Most species live below the shore and are found as washed-up skeletons, but a few live between the tides. Bivalves are safe from ragworms inside their shells but fall prey to more persistent and specialized predators. The burrowing starfish *Astropecten* seizes any bivalves, worms and sea urchins that it encounters, and a sea snail *Natica*, sometimes called the necklace shell, has a huge foot which is used to force a way through the sand. When the necklace shell finds a tellin or other bivalve it seizes hold with its foot and, drilling a neat hole in the shell, removes the contents. The presence of *Natica* under a beach is given away by a scattering of bivalve shells on the surface, each with a hole about one millimetre (0.04 inch) in diameter and tapering from the outside. There is also the netted dogwhelk which ploughs over firm mud, an environment that the common dogwhelk cannot tolerate. Small common whelks (*Buccinum*) may also be found on these shores where they feed on cockles, but mature individuals usually live below the tideline.

When the beach is covered by the tide, it becomes the hunting ground of fishes that move in from the sublittoral zone. In particular there are the flatfishes which appear regularly on our menus: lemon sole, Dover sole, plaice, flounder and dab. Adult flatfish live in deep water but their offspring drift inshore to develop. The baby flatfish looks like an ordinary round-bodied fish but, as it grows up, the body flattens and one eye migrates around the head so that it lies next to the other eye. Lying against the sand, flatfish are very difficult to see and their camouflage is improved by an ability to change colour to match the background. The Mediterranean flounder (*Bothus podas*) can make a good match with a chess-board.

In clear, shallow water, small plaice can be seen darting ahead of the naturalist as he wades carefully forwards. An occasional tickle underfoot will show that they have a preference for hiding under a solid object. The food of these flatfish is the protruding parts of worms and bivalves. The lemon sole eats fanworms and sand masons. It raises its head off the sand, watches for the worm's tentacles to unfold, and pounces. The loss of its tentacles does not harm the worm too much. It can grow a new set, so the fish is cropping a constantly renewed source of food, rather than hunting in the normal sense.

Above: When cleaned of sand, the ugly sea mouse shows brilliant iridescent colours

69

The sandeels (*Ammodytes*) are very important members of the fish community that patrols the flooded beach. They swim in shoals and, when disturbed, burrow into the sand by digging with their spoon-shaped lower jaws. Some sandeels remain buried in the sand when the tide goes out. Although most sandeels are no more than 22 centimetres (9 inches) long, they play a large part in the economy of the sea. They feed on the eggs and larvae of many marine animals and small crustaceans. In turn, their huge shoals form the diet of important food fishes such as young cod, herring and haddock. They are also taken by puffins, guillemots and terns.

A few other fishes are exclusive to sand and mud. Apart from the inconspicuous sand goby, there is a prickly threat to the unwary called the lesser weever (*Trachinus vipera*). This fish buries itself in the sand with eyes and mouth protruding,

ready to pounce on shrimps and small fish. The black dorsal fin is also left exposed and as the spines on the fin are poisonous, the lesser weever is a hazard to paddlers. The stargazers also lurk in the sand and mud. Like the weevers, its eyes are at the top of the head, inspiring the name. The stargazer's mouth is wide and upturned like a bulldog enabling it to snap up small animals attracted to a worm-like lure on the tongue. Also equipped with poisonous spines, stargazers are made doubly dangerous by electric organs around the eyes which can deliver an unpleasant 50-volt shock. However, neither weever nor stargazer is as nasty as the stonefish of tropical waters. Uglier even than the stargazer, the stonefish (*Synanceja verrucosa*) also plays a waiting game but delivers through its 13 dorsal spines one of the most dangerous of all venoms. Death often follows several hours of agony and, if it does not ensue,

Above : One of the few starfishes to live above low tide, this species, Astropecten auriantacus, burrows through sand in search of worms and shellfish
Top right : An elephant tusk shell is a rare and interesting find on the beach
Bottom right : Sandeels sometimes remain on the beach at low tide and dig into the sand

recovery is a slow process which may take months of convalescence.

Sandy and muddy shores do not have the obvious zonation of a rocky shore. The variation in animal communities is based on how exposed the shore is to the waves, and how fine the sand or mud is. Sandhoppers live in the dry sand at the top of the beach and, farther down, there is a damp zone roughly equivalent to the wrack-covered zone of rocky shores. Here, there is an isopod crustacean *Cirolana* which lives just under the surface, along with the cockles, lugworms and tellins. Lower down comes the equivalent of the oarweed zone. It is inhabited by heart urchins, razorshells, elephant tusk shells (*Dentalium*), rare in temperate waters but common in the tropics, and the masked crab (*Corystes cassivelaunus*); the last is not common above the low-tide mark. It digs down until only the tips of its long antennae protrude above the surface. These are fringed with bristles that make a tube through which the crab pumps water for breathing. Muddy shores have a zonation with ragworms, dogwhelks, gapers, sand clams (*Macoma*) and the burrowing crustacean *Corophium* up the shore and peacock worms, razorshells and fan mussels near the bottom.

A further variation in animal communities is due to wave exposure and the size of particles composing the beach. For instance, some animals cannot survive in soft mud while others cannot survive in clean sand. Permanent burrows do not survive well on a wave-washed beach but the common ragworm makes a mucus-lined tube in mud. Variety is also given to a muddy or sandy beach by occasional stones, flotsam and groins which attract rocky shore animals such as mussels, barnacles and periwinkles.

Overleaf: A river estuary at low tide reveals mudbanks which are the home of marine animals capable of surviving in fresh water

Estuaries

An estuary is a special kind of shore. It has the properties of other shores and its inhabitants have to face all the problems of drying and heat but they are also confronted by a further important problem. Estuarine animals have to survive brackish water, that is, water of reduced salinity. The river at the head of an estuary is continually discharging fresh water into the sea. In the typical funnel-shaped estuary the fresh and salt waters mix in such a way that it is difficult to tell where river ends and sea begins. The mixing is usually complex. Fresh water is lighter so it flows over the sea water; the great rivers of the world discharge so much fresh water that the sea is diluted many kilometres from the coast. On the other hand, the estuary of a small river is more like a narrow bay and the sea is the dominant influence. Mixing of fresh and salt water is further modified by the action of the tide. A high spring tide, for example, dams up the river and salt water pushes far inland. All these factors make the estuary a dynamic habitat, which demands resourceful and flexible characteristics of its inhabitants.

Many estuaries are characterized by large areas of mudflats and saltmarsh formed by the silt brought down by the rivers. The fauna and flora of estuaries are similar to those of sandy and muddy shores but modified for salinity changes, and, to a lesser extent, for the rapid changes in temperature resulting from the extra heat or chill of river water. Few algae penetrate far up estuaries except for the green weed *Enteromorpha intestinalis*. Animals may appear to be few because they are hiding under the mud but some kinds are present in abundance. These are the species that can adapt to the changes in salinity. Some of the mid-shore animals occur lower down the shore because they need to be wetted by fully salt water at each tide and submersion in brackish water is no substitute. Nearly all estuarine animals have moved in from the sea, with very few coming down from the rivers. An exception is the worm *Tubifex* which lives in masses so large that they may even colour the mud red. *Tubifex* worms are commonly found in polluted rivers where they can survive on a minimum of oxygen although a few of their species live in brackish water.

Estuarine animals can be divided into two kinds. Those that resist brackish water and those that adapt to it. Resisters include barnacles and bivalve molluscs that can close their shells when the water gets too fresh. Mussels close their shells as a temporary expedient but also adapt well to fresh water. They are flourishing in the increasingly fresh water behind the dams that the Dutch have erected around their coasts. The mussel's

success comes from its ability to tolerate the loss of salts from the body. The salt concentration in its tissue fluids reduces until it is the same as that in the surrounding water. Other estuarine animals such as the shore crab survive in estuaries, maintaining a relatively high salt concentration in their bodies by means of an efficient excretory system. Osmosis, the tendency of water to percolate through porous barriers, causes the flooding of tissues with water when the animal is immersed in fresh water but the crab compensates by excreting it again.

The amphipod crustacean *Gammarus* has a zonation of species up the estuary as neat as the shore zonation of the periwinkles. The zonation is based on the species' ability to survive different salinities. *Gammarus locusta* lives in the sea and does not move far up estuaries. It is gradually replaced by *Gammarus salina* which is replaced in

Above: Low tide reveals flat sandy beaches around the island of Texel. Under the bare surface live enormous populations of shellfish

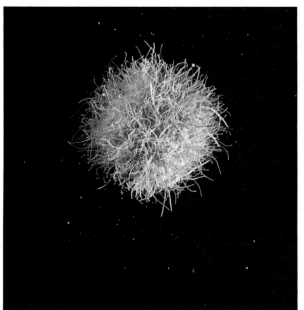

op right : Amphipod
rustaceans live in
rackish estuarine
ater. Here the male
lasps the female
3ottom right : Tubifex
orms can occur in
uch huge numbers that
hey colour the mud red

turn by *Gammarus zaddachi*, both of these being brackish water species. Further upstream they give way to *Gammarus duebeni*. This crustacean is the master of the estuary as it can survive rapid changes in salinity. However, it may be driven out of fresh water by *Gammarus pulex*, the so-called freshwater shrimp that is so abundant in lakes and rivers. It ousts *Gammarus duebeni* because the latter breeds more slowly in fresh water and cannot hold its own with the freshwater shrimp which is better adapted and provides overwhelming competition.

Behaviour also plays a part in survival in estuaries. We have seen how the laver spire snail feeds by the device of floating up the shore then working its way back down to the sea. In an estuary, it would be in danger of being carried into fatally fresh water. However, it saves itself by becoming less active as salinity drops and at a

critically low salinity, it stops floating, drops to the bottom, where the water is more salty, and closes its operculum. Here it lies, immune to fresh water, until the tide comes in again. Another abundant animal in these changeable waters is the common ragworm (*Nereis diversicolor*). It feeds either by trapping minute particles or by chewing larger prey. Large numbers gather to prey on the *Tubifex* worms. *Nereis diversicolor* can survive, like *Gammarus duebeni*, in either fresh or salt water but is rarely found at such extremes. At the seaward end of the estuary it cannot face competition from other ragworms and in fresh water it fails to breed. Like so many marine animals its eggs give rise to minute larvae. These would be swept out to sea and lost if they floated like those of barnacles or mussels. Instead, knowing their place, they hide in the mud until they become fully mature.

Mangrove Swamps

Long stretches of tropical and subtropical coasts are isolated effectively from the sea by strips of mangrove swamp. These are the equivalent of the saltmarshes in temperate latitudes, being mud-flats that have been invaded and stabilized by plants. The most obvious difference between saltmarsh and mangrove swamp is in density of vegetation. A saltmarsh is an open flat with low growing grasses and herbs, and a mangrove swamp is an impenetrable forest of trees. Mangrove trees grow in mud which is covered by sea water at high tide. The roots grow from a sort of inverted candelabrum of down-curving branches called rhizophores or prop roots. These form a dense thicket which impedes tidal currents and hastens the deposition of mud. The composition of mangrove swamps varies little from Florida to Queensland as most of the trees have seeds which are dispersed by ocean currents. Formation of the swamp starts with colonization by the red mangrove *Rhizophora mangle*. Its seeds sprout while still on the tree and drop into the mud where they develop rapidly or are carried by the sea to colonize new places. Black mangroves and white mangroves usually grow on the landward side of the red mangrove, often with turtle grass, cord grass and various palms.

The tangle of roots and the organically rich mud provides shelter and food for many animals, including many waders that migrate from cooler regions, often flying huge distances to warmer latitudes for the winter. Mussels, oysters and barnacles attach themselves to the prop roots and worms live in the mud, but the most spectacular inhabitants of these swamps are the hordes of crabs. Several kinds are known as mangrove crabs. There is a hermit crab *Scylla serrata* that

Left : Mangrove trees perch on their curving prop roots
Right : A male fiddler crab displays with an enormous claw. The small claw is used for feeding

makes holes as big as a rabbit burrow. Another mangrove crab is *Aratus pisoni* of tropical American shores. It has sharp claws for climbing mangrove trunks and survives long periods out of water by letting a thin trickle of water flow out of the gill chamber over the surface of its body and back to the gills, thereby avoiding desiccation and oxygenating its body.

The surface of the mud seethes with fiddler crabs, which are also found on sandy beaches. The fiddlers feed on mud and sand which they pick up with their pincers and transfer to their mouthparts where edible organic material is scraped off each grain. The cleaned grains are bundled into a ball and ejected, covering the surface of the mud or sand with little balls. When disturbed the crabs scuttle to safety, each to its own burrow. Male fiddler crabs have to feed with only one pincer because the other is a huge appendage that dwarfs

the rest of the crab. This claw is brightly coloured and is used in displaying to other crabs. Each species has its particular display which involves semaphore-signalling with the large pincer. These brightly coloured, waving claws are, of course, eye-catching both to other crabs and the human observer. So stereotyped is the display that fiddler crab species can be identified by the form of the display. Some fiddlers also call by rapping the large pincer on the ground or vibrating their legs. The purpose of the displays is the same as that of a bird's singing. The crab is proclaiming its ownership of a patch of mud to other males. If the signal is ignored, a fight ensues and the intruder is driven away. At the same time, the flashing colours of the displays also attract the female fiddlers. They promenade past the males who are driven to even more frantic displays in the hope of attracting a mate.

Above: Oysters growing on the prop roots of a mangrove tree

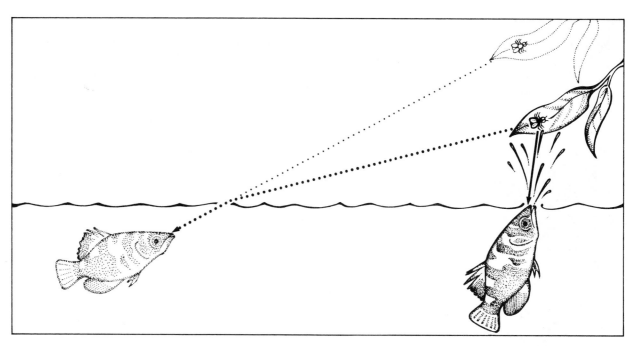

Some remarkable fishes also live among the mangroves. The archerfish (*Toxotes jaculatrix*), which ranges from India to Australia, feeds on insects by knocking them off their perches. On spotting an insect, the archerfish manoeuvres under it and violently compresses its gill covers to squirt water through a tube formed by the tongue resting against a groove in the roof of the mouth. The force behind the jet is sufficient to propel water droplets one metre or more and, if the fish misses, it can fire repeated bursts until the insect is dislodged and falls to the surface of the water and the waiting archerfish.

The falling tide will reveal another fish among the mangroves. The mudskipper is a peculiar looking creature with a large head, eyes on stalks and leg-like pectoral fins which are used as crutches for crawling over the mud at low tide. There are several kinds of mudskipper ranging from West Africa across the Indian Ocean to the Pacific and they even show a pattern of zonation among the mangroves. Some live on mud on the seaward side on the mangroves, others live in more estuarine conditions and stay near water, while a third group actually climbs trees. Of the last, some species are restricted to the prop roots but others have the paired pelvic fins modified to form a sucker that enables them even to negotiate vertical trunks.

Mudskippers can spend some time out of water but they frequently return to pools of water or burrow in the mud to moisten the skin and fill their gill chambers with fresh water. Like the fiddler crabs, mudskippers defend territories on the mud by displaying. Some species display by raising their dorsal fins, others do 'press-ups', and one species flips itself into the air so that, for a split second, it is standing vertically on its tail.

79

The Strand-line

Most things that reach the seashore stand a reasonable chance of ending up on the strand-line. This is the line of debris that runs parallel to and a little above the high-tide mark. It consists mainly of seaweed but may include almost any object connected with the shallow seas, the littoral zone, with passing ships or even with the open oceans. There is no greater medley of ill-considered trifles in the world, unrivalled even by the kitchen middens of prehistoric man or the municipal rubbish tips of the present day. In it we may find broken boxes, wood, cork, empty cans, shells, seabird feathers or bones, pumice from volcanic eruptions, potato peelings, items of clothing, the rubbish from ships and from seaside towns, the dried remains of a wide variety of sea animals – the list is endless. Unfortunately, the main constituent nowadays is empty plastic containers that do not rot and pile up year after year.

Another common constituent of the strand-line, in some parts of the world, is balls of fibrous vegetable material. A surprise occurrence is recorded for 14 October 1949 when the shore around Torbay, in southwest England, was found in the morning to be clothed in green. A belt 3 metres (10 feet) wide was found above the high-tide mark made up of tens of millions of green balls averaging 2.5 centimetres (1 inch) diameter. This curious flotsam turned out to be the matted green threads of an alga, *Cladophora repens*, seldom washed up on the shores of England but common enough in the Mediterranean. Similar balls of vegetable matter are sometimes found on lake shores as well, and in the Mediterranean and on the coasts of Australia, a marine flowering plant, *Posidonia*, produces a similar phenomenon, because the rolling action of the current rubs off

its fibrous remains. These and others like them have been called aegagropila, meaning goat-ball, after the balls of hair that are found in the stomachs of goats and other hoofed animals.

Anything that reaches the littoral zone may end up on the strand-line provided it has some hard parts that will resist total desiccation. This normally excludes jellyfishes which are sometimes stranded between the tidemarks and disintegrate into the 90 per cent water composing their bodies. One notable exception is a sort of jellyfish, although actually one of the siphonophores, known as *Physalia* or the Portuguese man-o'-war. It consists of a colony of polyps one of which forms a large bladder or float. The other polyps are of three kinds: the digestive polyps, solely concerned with feeding the whole colony, the reproductive polyps, and the long trailing tentacles, up to 10 metres (33 feet) long armed with stinging cells. The float is coloured blue with tinges of carmine. Its predominant colour has earned this siphonophore the nickname 'bluebottle' in some parts of the world. Its other popular name refers to a resemblance between the shape of the bladder, as it floats on the surface of the sea, and the shape of old Portuguese warships.

Physalia belongs to the warmer waters of the globe, although persistent winds occasionally carry it onto temperate shores. There the colonies readily disintegrate, like the true jellyfishes, except for the walls of the float which harden in the air and become durable relics of its presence.

The noun 'strand' refers to the shore between tidemarks. As a verb, it has two meanings, to drive ashore or to be left behind by the ebbing tide. Both are appropriate for the flora and fauna of this part of the shore. The exact position of the strand-line tends to fluctuate as the high-water of spring

Left: A debris of logs thrown up by wind and tide at Sitka, in Alaska

tides passes to High Water Neaps and back again to High Water Springs within a fortnight. However, the distance between the water's edge and the collection of bric-a-brac of the strand-line remains fairly constant.

Apart from the curious wreckage of land and sea, the strand-line above all contains seaweed torn from its anchorage by gales. The mass of seaweed to be found is most interesting for the small animals living in or on it, for it is here on the strand-line that the terrestrial and marine worlds commingle as nowhere else on the continents or the oceans. Its living inhabitants include small worms related to earthworms, seaweed flies and sandhoppers. All are scavengers. The first two are terrestrial animals gaining an easy living from the actions of the sea. Sandhoppers are marine animals which invade the land to pick up an equally easy living on the land's edge. By far the most interesting are the seaweed flies and the sandhoppers, if only because they are the most obvious, by reason of their vast numbers, and for the nuisance they can cause.

The seaweed flies are tiny, 4 millimetres (0.15 inch) long, with absurdly short antennae. They rise in swarms from the strand-line when it is disturbed by the waves or by the feet of passers-by. Sometimes they migrate in swarms at low tide, usually downwind and parallel to the coast, for no known reason, normally flying a foot or so off the ground. It has been suggested they are moving to new breeding grounds, the migrations being touched off by warmth and possibly overcrowding.

First impressions of these flies might suggest that their navigating sense was poor. Aided, it seems, by a following wind, they undertake mass suicide flights of anything up to 60 kilometres (37 miles) only to end up on the lantern of a lighthouse or the windowpanes of buildings well inland. A few years ago a pattern, if not an explanation, was found for this strange behaviour. These swarms were observed to home in on certain places to assemble, choosing shops, especially drug stores, perfumiers, garages and particularly dry cleaners. The one common element in all these places is the use of trichlorethylene. In one instance a swarm of the flies entered a watch-repairer's shop. There seemed to be no reason for this until it was noticed that the swarm was particularly attracted by one small bottle of trichlorethylene which was being used for cleaning delicate mechanisms.

There are several species of seaweed flies, widely distributed and all very similar. They seem to be most numerous in temperate regions, possibly because of the self-heating properties of rotting heaps of seaweed in these regions. As the seaweed becomes composted it gives out a slime which is highly nourishing for the fly larvae, so the whole life-cycle of the fly can normally be passed in or around the seaweed of the strand-line. One of the more important characteristics of these flies, which makes their peculiar habits possible, is that the adults are greasy and the surface of their bodies water-repellent. When immersed in water, far from drowning, they bob up to the surface and, unusual in flies, they can even take off from the surface of water.

Sandhoppers, sometimes called sand fleas or beach fleas, are small crustaceans that also feed on the strand-line, taking plant and animal food without discrimination. They only come to our notice if we lift a mass of decaying seaweed when swarms will scatter in all directions. They can jump distances seventy-two times their own length, by the simple expedient of suddenly straightening their naturally bent body, at the same time pushing off with the rear three pairs of legs.

One or more species of sandhopper seem to inhabit sandy beaches everywhere in the world. Although so small, their impact is great from sheer weight of numbers. They are probably all species of the family Tilitridae and all are scavengers, leading much the same lives keeping the beaches clean. They break up the seaweed eating it small piece by small piece, or clean down to the bone any decaying flesh of a fish cast up by the waves.

They belong to the group of crustaceans known as amphipods, from the Greek words *amphi* meaning both and *pous* meaning foot or leg. This indicates that they have both swimming and walking legs. The body itself is divided into a number of similar segments and in front carries a pair of eyes, a pair of antennae and a pair of

antennules. Sandhoppers are flattened from side-to-side but walk upright, not like some related crustaceans similarly shaped that wriggle on their sides, pushing themselves along using their rear legs.

The great majority of the very numerous kinds of crustaceans are marine. Some live in fresh water and only a very few live on land, the wood-louse or sowbug being a familiar example. Sand-hoppers are not strictly shore animals. They seem almost to be in process of passing from a marine to a terrestrial life. They burrow in the sand under the seaweed of the strand-line, leaving it when food becomes scarce to find fresh feeding grounds. Such a scarcity of food is probably the result of their enormous numbers. As somebody once remarked, they are found not in millions but in cartloads.

The strand-line must offer a habitat which keeps predation to a minimum because enormous numbers, as evidenced in sandhoppers, are usually a result of high breeding rates. Sandhoppers, or at least those of the genus *Talitrus*, have four broods of seventeen young in a year, and their life-span is between a year and eighteen months. This is a relatively slow breeding rate for crusta-ceans, so presumably there is a high survival rate in this genus.

Sandhoppers are nocturnal and burrow every morning in the dry sand beneath the strand-line. The females remain in their burrows while carrying eggs or young in their brood pouch, emerging only in the evening. This, as well as the numbers in which they exist has been vividly portrayed years ago in Paley's *Natural Theology*:

Walking by the sea-side, on a calm evening, upon a sandy shore, with an ebbing tide, I have frequently remarked the appearance of a

dark cloud, or rather very thick mist, hanging over the edge of the water, to the height perhaps of half a yard, and of a breadth of two or three yards, stretching along the coast as far as the eye could reach, and always retiring with the water. When this cloud came to be examined, it proved to be nothing else than so much space filled with young Shrimps, in the act of bounding into the air from the shallow margin of the water, or from the wet sand. If any motion of a mute animal could express delight, it was this; if they had meant to make signs of their happiness, they could not have done it more intelligibly. Suppose then, what I have no doubt of, each individual of this number to be in a state of positive enjoyment, what a sum, collectively, of gratification and pleasure we have here before our view.

It was probably hunger rather than ecstasy that inspired the sandhoppers since they sometimes range far down over the shore in search of food. This reveals a curious paradox, related to their semi-marine nature: that they need the presence of salt in the sand yet can drown if submerged for long periods in water. They are thus confined more or less to the strand-line. If they wander inland they are lost. To go the other way, into the water, is to court death by drowning.

Birds of the Seashore
Quiet undisturbed shores are a favourite haunt of the birdwatcher. The shore itself is a superb setting and it is also a rich feeding ground for many bird species which, at certain times, gather into huge flocks. The small animals we have considered in earlier chapters make a readily available diet for casual visitors such as crows and herons

and for specialists like the many waders. So birds are important as predators in the shore food web. There are also a number of offshore feeders that can be watched from beach or cliff, but do not belong to the shore community. These include the terns that plunge for small fish and shrimps, the cormorants that dive deep, some kingfishers that haunt coasts, and the North American brown pelican which fishes in seas and estuaries.

However, with an amphibious animal like a bird, it is not easy to draw a hard line between feeding at sea and feeding on the shore. Eider ducks usually feed at sea but they also pluck intertidal animals from weed-covered rocks. The American white ibis (*Eudocimus albus*) digs in the mud of mangrove swamps for fiddler crabs and the European spoonbill (*Platalea leucorodia*) sometimes eats tellins. The real shorebirds are the gulls and the waders, although some of these spend their lives inland. Of the passerine or perching birds which make up the majority of the bird world, few have found a living on the shore. The pipits are found on shores around the world and some of the ovenbirds (*Furnarius*) feed among floating kelp mats on the coast of Chile.

The gulls eat anything. Some live inland and have a diet of insects, others fish in deep waters but the majority are the familiar scavengers and scroungers of the seaside. They are opportunists, pouncing on anything live or dead that they can handle with their strong, slightly hooked bills. The bodies of washed-up animals attract a throng of jostling, screaming gulls and individuals pick over masses of dead seaweed for anything that may be lurking underneath. Two special feeding techniques have been developed which give the gulls an air of intelligence. The black-headed gull (*Larus ridibundus*) for example 'foot-paddles', running on the spot as it were, in shallow puddles on the beach, then jumps smartly one pace back so that it can seize any animals that have been disturbed from the sand. Herring gulls (*Larus argentatus*) smash mussels and crabs by flying with them and dropping them from a height. However, this behaviour is shown to be instinctive and quite lacking in intelligent direction, because a gull will repeatedly fly up and drop a shell on soft mud, ignoring the hard rocks nearby.

The waders are a group of about a dozen families of birds specialized for life on the seashore. Indeed, these birds are collectively called shorebirds in America. Some, such as the killdeer (*Charadrius vociferus*) of America and the lapwing (*Vanellus vanellus*) of Europe, live inland. Many of the shoredwellers breed inland then migrate to the shores for the winter. Characteristically, waders or shorebirds have a camouflaged plumage

that makes them difficult to pick out, especially when they are incubating eggs in a shallow ground nest. They are long-legged runners, with bills ranging from the short stub of the ringed plover (*Charadrius hiaticula*) to the long, slender bill of the curlew. The many variations in bill size and shape reflect the diversity of feeding habits within this group. There may be several species of waders feeding along one stretch of beach, but their bill differences prevent them from competing for food.

Most waders are found on sand or mud, and rocky shores are not a favourite feeding ground, although oystercatchers and *Calidris maritima*, the purple sandpiper, feed here. Oystercatchers would be better named 'musselcatchers' as their main foods are mussels, along with cockles, crabs, periwinkles, limpets and worms. The individual oystercatcher is conservative in its choice of food:

Above: Herring gulls home in on the shore, looking for anything edible, dead or alive

some feed on crabs which they kill by flipping them on their backs and delivering a stab to the brain; others prefer mussels and have two ways of dealing with them. Mussels that are firmly attached by their byssal threads are attacked when covered by shallow water. The mussels are open then, and a blow from the bill will sever the adductor muscles linking the shells, so rendering the mussel helpless. Mussels that can be dislodged are carried to a firm piece of ground and the closed shells are hammered open. The oyster-catcher always hammers the weakest part of the shell and when it has been breached, the bill is again used to cut the adductor muscles.

Using the bill as a hammer is taken farther by the crab plover (*Dromas ardeola*) of Arabian and Indian coasts which batters shellfish and crabs. However this is only one of many feeding adaptations. Most waders can be seen probing sand and

mud, their bills dipping in and out like the needle of a sewing machine. Examination of the beach after the birds have gone reveals rows of stitch marks in the sand and perhaps a more disordered hole where an animal has been ousted.

There is a general correlation between the length of the bill and the kind of food that is taken. Short-billed waders like the dunlin (*Calidris alpina*) must be content with animals living on or near the surface, such as *Hydrobia* snails and amphipod crustaceans. The sanderling (*Calidris alba*) runs up and down the tide's edge picking up animals stranded by receding waves. The turn-stone usually feeds like other short-billed waders, but gets its name from the habit of turning over pebbles and seaweeds to find animals underneath. The longer-billed sandpipers, like the redshank (*Tringa totanus*) and the American yellowlegs (*Tringa melanoleuca* and *Tringa flavipes*), dig

Overleaf: Sooty terns nest in their hundreds among low-lying plants just behind the shores

deeper and can reach tellins or seize ragworms and lugworms when these worms move up their burrows. The waders with the longest probe are the curlews which can reach down to the gapers but they also pick periwinkles off the surface of rocks.

Among these probing and picking waders, there are some with strange bills and unusual habits. The long-legged avocets (*Recurvirostra*) sweep their upcurved bills from side to side, like a scythe, to catch small swimming animals and the spoon-billed sandpiper (*Eurynorhynchus pygmeus*) of eastern Siberia has a flattened tip to the bill, as its common name suggests. It feeds by filtering edible matter from mud. The strangest wader of them all is the wrybill plover (*Anarhynchus frontalis*) of New Zealand. Its bill twists to the right and is used to probe among pebbles. However, why it needs a bent bill to do a job that the turnstone does with a straight bill is still not known.

Estuaries and saltmarshes are the home of waterfowl or wildfowl, that is ducks and geese. The shelduck (*Tadorna tadorna*) feeds mainly on *Hydrobia* snails, following them up and down the tide. The mallard (*Anas platyrhynchos*) and teal (*Anas crecca*) eat *Hydrobia* but they also visit saltmarshes to eat the seeds of sandwort and cord-grass. In winter the saltmarshes are the haunts of geese which feed on eelgrass in particular. The disappearance of eelgrass in the 1930s hit many geese very hard and today all the shorebirds are threatened by the wholescale reclamation and pollution of estuaries and saltmarshes.

Beachcombing

There is treasure to be found on the shore and there are people who make a practice of looking for it. They are known as beachcombers. Originally, beachcomber was a name used in America for a long wave rolling in from the Pacific Ocean. It has also been used for someone who settles on a Pacific island and earns a living by pearl-fishing and the like, or for one who loafs about the wharfs and beaches. More commonly, we think of a beachcomber as somebody who walks along the beach with his eyes on the ground looking for what may turn up in the way of coins, jewellery and the other valuable flotsam and jetsam of the high seas. Flotsam and jetsam, in modern usage, cover the miscellaneous items washed up by the sea on the beaches. Flotsam means strictly floating wreckage, jetsam means goods thrown overboard from a ship in distress, to lighten the load. Those are the definitions in law but the two words in combination are used for anything washed ashore.

Most people who comb the beaches are casual sleuths, either people on holiday or those with naturalist tendencies interested more in the animals and plants that may be left by the ebbing tide. Among the common run of marine treasures are such things as empty shells, attractive for their shapes and colourings. Then there are the mermaid's purses, a name originally applied to the dark brown to black, leathery-looking, oblong cases with a 'horn' at each corner. These are the egg-cases of skates, fish with a cartilaginous skeleton related to sharks. The small, similar egg-cases, amber-coloured and with a long tendril at each corner, are dogfish egg-cases, more rarely washed up because the tendrils become entangled in seaweeds below the strand-line. On tropical shores more elaborate, sometimes spirally twisted egg-cases laid by other sharks or rays are found.

Starfishes do not properly belong to the beaches. They belong more to the shallow seas beyond low-tide mark, although some forms may be found among pebbles or under seaweeds in the lower reaches of the beach uncovered at low-water spring tides. However, no artist sketching the beach would dream of excluding a starfish, and rightly so because dead or moribund starfishes are often among the jetsam. Perhaps even more attractive are the empty shells of sea-urchins with their repetitive patterns. Sea-urchins, like starfishes, are very ancient animals, their fossils being among some of the oldest known and little changed in appearance. Fossil or present day, all sea-urchins, globular, heart-shaped or, like the sand dollars, flattened, are attractive to the casual collector. So are the fossil sea-urchins, known as shepherd's crowns in some parts of England, where they are picked up and treasured by people with no other interest in geology or zoology. Even prehistoric man seems to have been fascinated by them. At least one skeleton of prehistoric man was disinterred with a circle of shepherd's crowns surrounding it. Either these fossil urchins were regarded by our early ancestors as magical, or else as attractive adornments of a burial.

For the more ardent naturalist, the root-like holdfasts of the large seaweeds, the kelps, torn from their attachment on the rock below low-water mark, shelter a variety of small animals such as sponges and sea-mats. The sea-mats go under the names of the moss animals: Bryozoa, or Polyzoa. Each sea-mat is a colony of tiny polypides, with each polypide in its separate box, the whole giving a lace-like pattern.

Marine zoology owes more than we normally suppose to the curiosity of beachcombers. Centuries ago there were no museums and very few books on natural history. The first museums were

merely piles of specimens in the houses of wealthy scholars and were little more than collections of curios. In the sixteenth century scholars finally began to turn their attention to these curios and in the natural history books of those times we see beautiful coloured plates showing all kinds of marine animals. Many of these simply showed the fishes caught on the lines or in the nets of regular fishermen. Anything unusual from that source easily found its way into a collection.

Another kind of jetsam was probably responsible for a number of ancient sea mysteries or sea legends. There was, for example, the legend of the kraken, a dialect Norwegian word referring to a monstrous 'fish'. Although the name originated in Norway, the animals that constituted the kraken legend were reported from a much wider area. It may have been too that the fabulous hydra said to have been killed by Hercules was also a squid, a

Above : Outsize flotsam, a giant baleen whale lies washed up on the shore. Whales sometimes run ashore when alive and die before they can get clear

relative of the octopus but with ten arms and a more torpedo-like body. Most squids are small, a few centimetres long but the kraken was something different. Squids included under this name were large, measuring ten metres or more with their tentacles outstretched. Man's first knowledge of the giant squids of the deep seas came from carcases washed ashore.

A near relative of the squid is the cuttlefish. Both are molluscs that have what remains of their shell inside them. The squid's shell is a thin, horny 'pen', shaped like an old-fashioned pen-nib. This is something seldom found on the beach. Much more common is the cuttlebone, the whitish limy material of which is often found wedged between the wires of small bird cages. Cuttlebone may be found on the shore at low tide singly or in their hundreds. Each is oval in outline, around 15 centimetres (6 inches) long and about 2 centi-

metres (o.8 inch) at the thickest, central part, with two horny flaps at one end. Cuttlebone floats, and at times long lines of cuttlebones can be seen at sea. Some of them probably make long journeys, carried around by the currents before being cast ashore.

One of the easiest ways of obtaining specimens of shipworm is by examining logs or other lumber cast up on the beaches. The shipworm is a long, worm-like mollusc with a shell reduced to two small pallets capable of rasping tunnels in wood. In former times, it attacked ships' timbers and some believe that the disaster to the Spanish Armada in the sixteenth century was less due to the attacks of the English than to the shipworms that had eaten the ships' hulls.

Another unintentional visitor from the open oceans to the seashore is the ship's barnacle. An ancient legend had it that the barnacle goose was

generated from the barnacle. Certainly, disregarding the matter of size, there is a strong similarity in both shape and colouring between the bird and the barnacle. Ship's barnacles are not infrequently cast ashore attached to pieces of waterlogged wood, even to wooden boxes, as well as to pieces of pumice or lumps of tar which, because of their porous structure, are light enough to float. No doubt the first ship's barnacles were discovered by man on dead trees that had drifted on the oceans and finally came ashore. They led to the Medieval legend of the barnacle goose growing from a barnacle.

The sea serpent is another mystery of the sea which, if it did not originate there, has been bolstered by items of flotsam and jetsam. Several of the most famous 'finds' on the shore, first alleged to be remains of a sea serpent, have later proved to be the highly decomposed and disintegrating carcases of large sharks, especially of the basking shark. On at least two occasions, large whales in an advanced stage of decay, the long bones of the lower jaw projecting from an unrecognizable mass of putrefying flesh, have been cast up on the beaches. The jawbones were thought by the finders to be the enormous fangs of some sea monster.

Zoologically speaking, the most valuable find by a beachcomber is the curious relative of the sea firs known as *Pelagohydra*. In 1902 an English-born zoologist, due to return home from New Zealand, was taking a last walk along the shore when suddenly he saw a curious rounded object about the size of a pingpong ball. He was about to put his heel on it and pass on when something caused him to stoop, pick it up and take a closer look. It was a marine animal, a colony of tiny polyps with part of the body expanded into a float. The odd thing is that this, at least until a few years ago, was the only specimen of *Pelagohydra* ever found. It clearly must exist in large numbers, but so far has escaped capture apart from this one stranded colony. The zoologist made no money out of it although he experienced intense satisfaction and a tremendous boost to his reputation.

A more numerous kind of flotsam and jetsam produced, or so the story goes, a far more epoch-making discovery. These are two kinds of bean, one the usual bean shape with a hard shiny skin, *Entada gigas*, and the other, *Mucuna urens*, disc-shaped with black rim running round most of its circumference. The first drifts over from the West Indies, the second from tropical America and both may be cast up on the shores of western Europe. It has been said that Columbus was

Above : Still alive but out of its element, a starfish has been evicted from its home by a storm
Top right : Strange objects appear on the strand-line. This is the skull of a dogfish
Bottom right : A sandhopper leaps across the sand in search of food

94

convinced of the existence of land to the westward from finding these beans on the shore.

Although almost all of human and marine life may be cast up on the strand-line, one of the most traditional beach treasures is ambergris. It floats and is often cast up on the shore, but, unfortunately for would-be treasure seekers, there is more false ambergris picked up than the real article. Lumps of candle-grease and carnauba wax, soap and suet are washed ashore and have all been mistaken for ambergris. This is not surprising because this valuable commodity has few outstanding characteristics by which it can be recognized. The name 'amber' is Arabic in origin and was originally used for the real product, but was later applied to fossil resin. The French eventually distinguished between the bogus yellow *ambre jaune* and the real *ambre gris*.

Ambergris occurs naturally in the intestine of the sperm whale and may be found floating on the sea or cast up on the shore. Lumps of ambergris are found in various sizes from quite small fragments to massive pieces over 50 kilogrammes (110 pounds) in weight. Ambergris is a dull, wax-like substance, varying in colour from greyish-white to very nearly black. In its natural state it has a peculiar, strong smell, but the longer it is kept the more agreeable the odour becomes.

Shores of the World

The pattern of wildlife on a seashore depends on many things. Although shores look rather alike from one part of the world to another, there are reasons why some animals and plants occur in one place and not another. The physical character of the shore is determined by local geology, currents and river sediments and they affect what can live there. Above all, however, climate and ocean currents working on a global scale have an overwhelming importance in deciding the composition of a shore community. Animals and plants exposed by the tides are susceptible to excessive heating, frosts and the physical scouring of ice, and they depend on currents to bring the nutrients needed to build up the intricate food web.

Climate always depends on the circulation of vast masses of air. Near the equator, air is heated and rises; at the poles it cools and sinks, so there is a continuous movement of air from poles to equator. This movement is distorted by the rotation of the Earth on its axis, so that air movement is deflected towards the right of its general direction in the northern hemisphere and to the left in the southern hemisphere. This is not the only force acting on air movement, and the result is a system of winds that can be grouped into the north-east and south-east trades running into the equatorial 'doldrums', and the westerlies flowing in opposite directions from the subtropical 'horse latitudes'.

The principal systems of prevailing winds set up water currents, in the same way as a storm sets up a swell, so there are ocean currents following roughly the tracks of the winds. In subtropical regions, there are 'gyres', huge circular movements of water. The seaweeds of the Sargasso Sea are caught in the middle of a gyre whose currents and winds carried Columbus to America. Equatorial currents are driven westwards by the trade winds, with a counter-current running between them, and to the north and south the West Wind Drifts move eastwards. South of America and Africa, winds and currents have an uninterrupted flow around the world and gave power to the clipper ships whose run between Europe and Australia took them around South Africa on the outward run and past Tierra del Fuego on the return.

The gyres are further deflected by the continental land masses and cause currents that run along their coastlines. These are important to shore life: in the North Atlantic, the Gulf Stream runs up the Florida coast, then crosses to Europe to bathe the north-west coasts of the continent. This makes the climate of the British Isles more equable than that of Labrador which lies on the same latitude but receives the cold Labrador Current from the Arctic. Other important currents include the cool Benguela Current running up the west coast of Africa and the Humboldt Current which branches off the West Wind Drift and cools the coast of Chile and Peru. It is this current that attracts the penguins of the equatorial Galapagos Islands.

An important part of ocean circulation is the upwelling and sinking of water masses. Where two masses of water meet, one must sink and, in doing so, will carry oxygenated water down for deep-sea creatures to breathe. At the Antarctic Convergence, cold, dense water sinks under warmer water from temperate latitudes. Conversely, divergence of water masses causes an upwelling of water. This brings nutrient materials for surface-dwelling plants and so is vital for productive food webs. Where a prevailing wind runs along the coast, surface water is pulled away from

Left: The average island paradise, conch shells and coconuts litter a tropical beach

97

the shore and water wells up. This happens along the west coast of South America and results in the massive populations of anchovetas, the small fishes on which the famous guano-producing birds live. Occasionally the Humboldt Current fails and is replaced by the warmer but poorer South Equatorial Current. Known as El Niño, disaster for the anchovetas and shore life follows this occurrence.

Thus climate, current, geology, wave exposure, tidal range and salinity all amalgamate to influence the formation of the seashore community. Described on the following pages are some examples of shores around the world to show how these factors in their various combinations affect the basic patterns of seashore life.

West Coast of Scotland

There was a time when the North Atlantic Ocean did not exist and North America and Europe were fused together. Then, some 60 million years ago, the two continents drifted apart, leaving a frayed coastline from Norway to Eire. Along these coasts, the hills and mountains run out to the sea to make a coastline of islands and deep fjords or sea lochs. The tearing of the rock masses also unleashed volcanoes which poured out molten material to make the islands of Mull, Arran, Skye, and Staffa

where the columns of solidified basalt form Fingal's Cave.

The ragged shape of the coastline makes the west coast of Scotland a place of contrasts. It is surprisingly warm because of the benign influence of the North Atlantic Current, or Gulf Stream, and palm trees grow in sheltered places. There are headlands which stand exposed to the gales sweeping in from the Atlantic, deep sheltered lochs and long beaches of pure, white sand. Among the small islands of the Hebrides, the three forms of topography alternate so that the zonation and appearance of the shore may alter appreciably within a short distance.

The exposed headlands are not a good hunting ground for the naturalist. The incessant swells remove all but the hardiest animals and plants, and there is no more than a skin of lichen and algae with a few barnacles or limpets and perhaps mussels and small periwinkles in the splash zone. A richer fauna is found only in rock pools where there are anemones, sea urchins and a few small fishes. Exploring the rocks can be a little hazardous with the surge and pull of the swell breaking over them.

The beautiful white beaches of the Hebrides have a rather desolate air as do most sandy shores. In a better climate they would be covered with

holidaymakers but, despite the warming of the North Atlantic drift, the Scottish summer is too unpredictable. The sand is not silica from weathered rock, but shell-sand composed of ground-up fragments of countless mollusc shells. The sand is blown inland to form dunes and the flat expanses of the *machair* (Gaelic for plain). Lime from the shell sand makes the *machair* very fertile, and the Hebrideans improve the humus content by spreading the surface with the remains of seaweed thrown up by winter storms.

By contrast with the headlands and the sands, the sheltered sea lochs have a rich intertidal habitat. They are sheltered from the swell, and the ebb of the tide is often restricted by narrows. At low tide the exposed rocks reveal a thick carpet of wracks beneath a line of orange lichens, while the land vegetation of grass or even woodland starts directly above.

The quiet watcher will see a variety of animals exploiting the wealth of shore creatures that have been uncovered. Herons stand sentinel at intervals, holding themselves rigid until unsuspecting prey comes within range, while, by contrast, oystercatchers, sandpipers, eiders and shelduck run about energetically searching for their main diet of periwinkles. The prize sighting is an otter, a mammal now rare or extinct in most parts of

Europe. However, it is still common in the Highlands of Scotland and frequently feeds along the shore, and will sometimes even swim to outlying islands. These fascinating creatures can be seen diving skilfully for fish and, on a lucky day, can also be seen bringing them to the shore to eat. To see an otter in the flesh is a chance treat, but it does leave easily identifiable traces in the form of piles of droppings deposited on rocks, and runways and sunbathing places on the top of the shore.

The west coast of Scotland is also the home of the grey or Atlantic seal and the common seal. About two-thirds of the world's grey seals live around the British Isles, of which half, about 28,000, gather around the Scottish west coast. They spend most of the year at sea but come ashore in the autumn to bear their white-coated pups on such isolated islands as North Rona, Gasker and the Monachs. Common seals live the year round in the shelter of sea lochs and small island groups. They bask on rocks exposed at low tide, and there give birth to the pups which must be able to swim before the tide returns to drown the birthplace.

The seashore has for long been important in the economy of the Hebridean islanders. Seaweeds and shells fertilize their smallholdings. In the past

Above : Gaunt cliffs and promontories on the west coast of Scotland resist the battering of Atlantic storms

*Above : Sheltered sea
lochs are the home of
the eider. The drakes
are gaudy in their
courtship plumage ; the
females are unobtrusive
for nesting
Above right : Plentiful
supplies of kelp are
used in many places to
manure impoverished
fields
Right : Grey seals
bicker on a remote
Hebridean shore
Far right : A little way
inland, eider chicks lie
in the soft down nest*

fish were caught as the tide ebbed and seals were taken for their oil and pelts, a cup of seal oil being quaffed as a tonic on a cold day! Some Hebrideans still make a living by collecting common periwinkles – the 'winkles' of the seaside stall – and by cutting 'kelp'. Kelp is the general name given to the seaweeds that have been harvested commercially in many parts of the world – from Scandinavia to the Falkland Islands. It was originally processed for its iodine content and today gelatinous agar is extracted for the manufacture of many things, from penicillin to ice cream. The Hebrideans cut the weeds with scythes as the fronds float at the water's edge and gather their harvest into compact rafts with an encircling rope.

The Baltic Sea

The Y-shaped sea that separates Scandinavia from eastern Europe was, at one time, a lake. When the Ice Age glaciers withdrew 8,000 years ago the Baltic Sea was joined to the North Sea by a wide opening across southern Sweden. Then the land rose and cut off the sea for 1,500 years before the Kattegat was breached again. Water now flows between Denmark and Sweden but the exchange is limited, and the waters of the Baltic Sea are distinct from the Atlantic Ocean outside the Kattegat. There is little tide; no more than 45

centimetres (18 inches) separate high and low water, and the salinity is much reduced. Fresh water flows in continually from rivers so that the salinity of the Baltic drops to as little as two parts per thousand in the Gulfs of Finland and Bothnia. This has a profound effect on the animals that can be found on Baltic shores. Even just inside the Skagerrak where the salinity has been reduced by only two parts per thousand, three-quarters of the species of some animal groups have disappeared. The marine animals are joined in the brackish water by some essentially freshwater animals such as roach, bream and pike, pond snails and the water hoglouse (*Asellus*) which can adjust to the extra salt. The animals that can tolerate brackish water thrive in the Baltic because the river water is rich in nutrients, and the remains of planktonic animals collect on the bottom as a rich, black mud.

The mud and sand flats of the Baltic are, therefore, rich habitats for those animals that can colonize them. Lugworms, for instance, can live in the Kiel Canal region where their blood contains half the concentration of salts as compared with North Sea lugworms. They make no attempt to maintain a high salt content but let it balance with the salinity of the water they live in.

The ragworms have a similar physiological tolerance for low salinities and one species, *Nereis virens*, can be a pest. It lives in huge numbers in the sands of the Kattegat of Denmark, where it grows as long as 70 centimetres (28 inches). These worms normally live unobtrusively under the sand but, at full moon in April, huge numbers come to the surface to spawn. They interfere with the activities of the fishermen but provide a feast for the seabirds.

Nereis diversicolor, the common ragworm, is also found in the Baltic but surprisingly it only penetrates to salinities of four parts per thousand, whereas in British waters it survives in water of less than one part per thousand. This is because the low temperature of Baltic sea water inhibits its breeding. By contrast, *Macoma balthica*, the Baltic tellin, lives in the Gulfs of Finland and Bothnia because it can survive freezing, but *Scrobicularia*, another mud-dwelling bivalve of brackish water, cannot withstand freezing and does not penetrate so far. Another difference in Baltic populations is that common whelks do not spread into the littoral zone as they do in Britain.

The Mediterranean Sea

English schoolchildren are taught how Julius Caesar's first expedition to Britain in 55 BC came near to disaster because the Romans knew nothing about tides. Caesar had beached his fleet on the

Above: A tideless sea washes on Bornholm, a large Danish island in the middle of the Baltic Above right: The peaceful Mediterranean. Pine forest comes down to the edge of a shore little affected by tide or waves

south coast and, while he struck inland, many of the ships were damaged or swept away by high tides and storms. The Romans had pulled their ships clear of the water no farther than was the practice in the Mediterranean, which being almost landlocked, has only minimal tides. Storms in the Mediterranean are also brief and rare when compared with those hitting the Atlantic coasts of Europe, and the swell never gets a chance to build up into huge rollers.

There is a considerable difference in the appearance of the shores between the Mediterranean and Atlantic coasts of Europe. On the Mediterranean side, the cliffs are not so eroded and, along the French coast, there are flat rock platforms covered with delicate corallines where the coast is exposed to clean, rough water. The form of the shore is also much more variable with areas of rocks, sand and mud mingling in one short stretch of shore.

Despite the lack of tides in the Mediterranean, there is still some zonation, although the littoral zone is very narrow and depends more on wetting by waves than on wetting by tides. At the top of the shore, land-dwelling tiger beetles live among sandhoppers (*Talitrus saltator*) which are splash zone crustaceans that have become almost independent of the sea. This sandhopper species may

even drown if kept submerged, and close relatives have become completely terrestrial. *Talitrus* sandhoppers have been the subject of experiment by Italian scientists. It has been observed that, as the sand dries out, the hoppers move down the shore into wet sand, navigating by the position of the sun. Each hopper has an instinctive knowledge of which course to steer when it needs to find damp sand. Hoppers collected at Rimini on the eastern coast of Italy still hopped in the same direction when transported to La Spezzia on the west, with disastrous results as they travelled inland instead of seawards.

The most noticeable zonation on Mediterranean coasts is below the shore. In clear water, a changing sequence of seaweeds can be seen stretching into deep water. Green seaweeds live in the shallowest water and red seaweeds live in the deepest. This is because the pigments of green weeds absorb red light which does not penetrate far into water, whereas red algae utilize blue light, which penetrates deepest, for their photosynthesis.

The Mediterranean makes a marked contrast with the similarly land-locked Baltic Sea. The Baltic Sea receives large amounts of water from rivers and, at the northern tips, is almost fresh. The Mediterranean also has an inflow of fresh

Overleaf: The rocky coast of Sardinia shows few signs of the zonation that is characteristic of the tidal Atlantic coasts

water but the sea is warmer and evaporation increases the salt concentration. Whereas the Baltic receives nutrient-rich sea water from the Atlantic, the Mediterranean only receives nutrient-poor surface water through the shallow Straits of Gibraltar. Furthermore, microscopic marine organisms do not decay into rich mud as in the Baltic. The result is that the Mediterranean is rather poor in marine life, and it has been suggested that the Straits of Gibraltar be deepened to improve Mediterranean fisheries by allowing in the richer ocean water. The most productive parts of the Mediterranean are around the river mouths where large amounts of silt are brought in. The region of the Nile delta is productive but the Adriatic Sea, lacking the input of large rivers, is poor.

Alarming changes are taking place around Mediterranean shores through Man's activities. The Aswan dam is preventing the life-giving silt from fertilizing the seas around the Nile delta, and the fauna of this region is now subject to immigration from the Red Sea. The Red Sea is slightly higher than the Mediterranean, so there is a slow flow of water through the Suez Canal, carrying tropical animals into the subtropical Mediterranean. For the first 60 years of the canal's existence very few animals made the journey because they were killed by the high salinity of the Great Bitter Lake and the very low salinity caused by Nile waters around Port Said. The canal is now much deeper and wider; its flow has increased so that the Great Bitter Lake's salt has been washed away while the Aswan Dam has at the same time reduced the flow of fresh water. The results have been dramatic; by 1929, 15 animals had traversed the canal, today about 150 species, including fishes, crabs, prawns and oysters, have migrated successfully.

The Nile coasts have probably benefited from the Red Sea immigrants which have become abundant enough to be fished commercially. Other places have been less lucky. The Mediterranean is a cess-pit for huge amounts of industrial waste and domestic sewage, and the natural processes of breakdown and cleaning cannot cope with this man-made effluent. The result is massive pollution and destruction of coastal life on a large scale, as has happened around Marseille. At the same time more and more tourists want holidays by the sandy beaches and hotels spring up to cater for them. Ecological destruction is often more to the land behind the shore than to the beaches, but this is not always the case as the plans to develop the Ebro delta illustrate.

The Ebro, the fourth largest river of the Mediterranean, empties its rich silt between

Above: Without the influence of tides, land plants can invade the sandy beach. The remains of coral are strewn in the foreground
Left: An octopus skulks just below the shore. It is not a danger to bathers
Right: The Spanish prawn is a justly famous delicacy on the Mediterranean seaboard

Valencia and Barcelona. The silt forms the basis of a food web which includes many commercially important animals. They include eels, grey mullet, sardines, cockles, mussels, *Paphia* carpet-shells, known locally as *almejas* and, above all, the Spanish prawn *Penaeus*. The marshes and lagoons in the delta are the home of some 250 kinds of birds, including flamingos. If the proposed development goes ahead, all this will be destroyed and the development itself will suffer from the instability of the delta coastline. So one of the richest and most exciting places around the Mediterranean shores will become a virtual desert.

The Coast of California

The Pacific Ocean was given the wrong name. Quite fortuitously it was first seen by European eyes on an unusually calm day. However, even on 'calm' days there is usually a heavy swell and because swells have a longer clear sweep in the Pacific than in the Atlantic, the western seaboard of North America is more wave battered than the eastern. The western seaboard is exposed to the prevailing westerly winds which blow across the huge expanse of ocean, generating huge trains of waves. Despite this long fetch, there is often shelter in the form of bays, offshore islands and, important in many places, beds of kelp just below the shore which deaden the swell. There is, in fact, a remarkable range of coastal forms from really exposed headlands, as at Point Lobos below Carmel Bay, to extreme shelter, as in San Francisco Bay.

The benign climate and the richness of seashore and marine life have attracted a number of marine biological stations to California coasts, but the most famous collector of California's sealife must be 'Doc' in John Steinbeck's *Cannery Row*. 'Doc' was liberally based on the character of Ed Ricketts who lived in Pacific Grove, near Monterey Bay, and who collaborated with Jack Calvin to produce *Between Pacific Tides*, a very readable handbook of shore life on the Pacific seaboard. Reading this excellent book, the European reader is struck, on the one hand, by the diversity and richness of California's shores and, on the other, by the familiarity of many of the animals. Diversity comes from the variety of habitats and the warm climate, for it is a general rule that the warmer the place the more animal species it harbours. However, intertidal species cannot stand too much heat and the abundance of species is aided by low tides in California occurring before the hottest part of the day and also by the protection of frequent fogs.

The familiarity of so many animals shows how cosmopolitan many seashore types are. A few are

107

exactly the same species as live on eastern and western Atlantic coasts, and many others are so similar that it takes a trained eye to distinguish the Pacific and Atlantic forms. A similarity with species on South African shores has also been noticed.

The exposure of Pacific shores to waves has given rise to wave-resistant species such as the California mussel, the purple starfish and purple urchin. California is unusual in the large populations of stalked goose barnacles, as opposed to acorn barnacles, and in a small anemone, *Anthopleura elegantissima*, which is so abundant in sheltered places that it may completely hide the underlying rock and may itself be hidden under a layer of gravel. Abalones are abundant where they are not collected, for they come farther up the shore than they do in Europe. Limpets are a good subject for the seashore observer in California. Many species are to be found, including 17 in the genus *Acmaea*. These limpets separate out on the shore in a zonation very similar to that of the European periwinkles.

The California coast has several spectacular large animals to interest the visitor. The largest is the grey whale which migrates down the coast from the north to give birth in protected bays and lagoons. Although not an intertidal animal, the grey whales swim so close to the shore that they are a considerable tourist attraction, now that their numbers are recovering after near extinction by hunters. The sea otter is another sublittoral animal that is recovering from overhunting. These animals are rarely seen ashore, although they give birth on land and sometimes come ashore to sleep. More typically, they sleep in the kelp beds with fronds of kelp wrapped around the body as an anchor. Sea otters are famous for their habit of floating on their backs and smashing open shellfish on a stone carried on the chest. Crabs, clams, whelks and abalones are dealt with in this way. Indeed, the sea otters have been charged with seriously reducing the numbers of abalones, and in some places have almost exterminated the *Strongylocentrus* sea urchins.

The shores are also enlivened by the presence of seals and sealions. The large and belligerent Steller's sealion breeds on Santa Rosa and San Miguel islands and the California sealion, of circus fame, occurs on a number of small islands. Point Lobos is named for the sealions whose barking is a familiar sound in the area. A few years ago, biologists studying sealions were surprised to find a small group of Pribilof fur seals among the sealions. They had migrated from Alaska, and their numbers are now increasing quite rapidly.

Above: The sprawl of San Francisco extends over the original shore. Little will be found living on this concrete strand
Top right: Californian sea-lions, scattered like flotsam along the shore keep clear of the surf but, at the same time, keep damp and cool
Bottom right: Sealion pups gather in groups before setting out to sea

The largest of the seals is the elephant seal, named for its huge, inflatable nose which hangs over the mouth. The biggest males weigh about 3,600 kilogrammes (7,900 pounds).

No description of California's shores is complete without reference to the grunion (*Leurestes tenuis*) whose strange breeding habits make it as much of a tourist attraction as the grey whale. This small fish spends most of its life below the shore, but comes out of the water to spawn on sandy beaches. At spring tides, when the water level is at its highest, millions of grunions leap out of the waves, either by day or night according to the habit of their species. Each female rapidly digs herself into the sand and lays a batch of eggs which are fertilized by a male. Spawning has to be accomplished just after high tide because a flowing tide tends to scour away the sand while an ebbing tide throws it up. In this way, the eggs get well-covered and develop during the next fortnight, when spring tides will again wash over them. The shaking imparted by the waves stimulates the eggs to hatch and the tiny fishes are washed out of the sand and swept down into the sea.

The Great Barrier Reef of Australia

The Great Barrier Reef is the name given to a series of coral reefs that lie off the tropical Queens-land coast and run from Cape York in the north to the Swain Reefs about 500 kilometres (310 miles) north of Brisbane. In fact, there is a series of barrier reefs, fringing reefs, islands and cays that follows the coast for 1,600 kilometres (1,000 miles). The reefs are 30–160 kilometres (20–100 miles) from the mainland shore, with the outer barrier effectively blocking the swell coming in from the Pacific. Within this complex system there are mangrove swamps, coral reefs that are exposed in places at low tide, wooded islands and cays of sand and shingle that build up or almost disappear in summer storms. There are also wide differences in salinity, shore topography, clarity of water and wave actions. All this variety is reflected in the shore communities, which are so diverse as to defy brief summary.

The coral reefs are formed of masses of live and dead corals, with sea fans, sponges and pink corallines. They are areas of outstanding beauty, both in form and colour. The outer margins are inhabited by the most solid corals but in some places the coral masses have been ground down to a coarse sand. The reefs are the home of the giant clam *Tridacna* which measures over 1.3 metres (4.3 feet) across the shell and weighs up to 200 kilogrammes (440 pounds). It lives in the coral, hinge downwards and gaping 'mouth' upwards.

*Right : The giant clam
lives in coral reefs,
showing a delicacy of
colour that belies the
deadweight of the shell
Below left : A barrier
reef forms a natural
breakwater for the
shore behind it. A
shallow covering of
water protects a myriad
of colourful creatures*

The edges of the fleshy mantle that line the rim of the shells are prettily coloured green and purple and contain microscopic algae called zooxanthellae. These absorb sunlight to produce sugars by photosynthesis, in the usual manner of plants. At the same time, they receive nutrients from the host clam, which benefits from the association by digesting some of the zooxanthellae.

The giant clam has been called the killer clam because it is alleged that divers or tourists walking over the reef at low tide get their legs caught in its gaping shells. The clam then snaps shut and the victim eventually drowns. Such stories are vivid but extremely unlikely. The clam can close up only very slowly and experienced biologists deny any fatalities. A much nastier encounter can be had with the cone shell *Conus*. The cones are among the most beautiful of all seashells and high prices are paid for some. Most live below the tides but a few can be found at low water. They are carnivores like the whelks, but the teeth at the tip of the proboscis are hollow and connected to a poison gland. Worms, marine snails and fishes are harpooned, paralyzed and eaten, and the poison is strong enough to cause severe injury and sometimes death in humans.

Coral is eaten by a number of animals, including boring bivalves, worms, sponges, sea cucumbers, parrotfishes and the crown-of-thorns starfish *Acanthaster planci*. In 1965, the crown-of-thorns, which has between 13 and 16 spine-covered arms, became extremely abundant on Green Island, part of the Great Barrier Reef. This was a favourite haunt of tourists and it soon became clear that the starfish were completely destroying the reefs. Because of the effect of a crown-of-thorns plague on the tourist industry and the rich food web of the coral reefs, biologists and conservationists became very worried, particularly when reef devastation was discovered in other parts of the world. Surveys were undertaken and attempts were made to destroy the starfish. It was suggested that the plague was caused by human interference but, it eventually became clear that huge increases in starfish numbers are a natural occurrence. Their numbers eventually dwindle, perhaps aided by the attacks of shrimps, fishes and other predators. Moreover, the reefs regrow much more quickly after devastation than was thought. Within 10–15 years of almost complete destruction of live coral, the reef will be back to normal.

Like other tropical shores, the Great Barrier Reef has large numbers of crabs, including ghost crabs and box crabs. *Scylla serrata*, the mud crab, skulks in its burrow among the mangroves at low tide while the other crabs are running about. This

Top left : The crown of thorns starfish eats corals and sometimes devastates reefs. Luckily the coral regrows quickly
Left : The mantis shrimp seizes small animals with jack-knife legs, in the same way as the more familiar praying mantis insect

Above : A mass of colourful, bizarre corals are exposed on the Great Barrier Reef of Australia

is prudent because it is edible and is often fished in Queensland. Sandy and muddy beaches have populations of dogwhelks, a few conches that have strayed from deeper water, long-bodied acorn worms and burrowing anemones. There are also mantis shrimps (*Squilla*) which live in burrows and, like the praying mantis insect, seize their prey with limbs in which the last joint snaps back against the next like the blade of a jack-knife. The limbs are often armed with sharp spines to help trap the prey. Mantis shrimps can give a human finger a nasty nip and cut other shrimps and fishes clean in two.

The Atlantic Coast of Florida

The seashore life of Florida is tropical. Although the State of Florida lies outside the Tropic of Cancer, the Florida Current, which is part of the Gulf Stream, brings tropical water along the Atlantic coast. From Miami, running in an arc towards the south-west, lies a chain of islands called the Florida Keys. They are the visible part of a submarine plateau that is covered by less than 100 metres (330 feet) of water and sometimes shoals to about a metre. Along the edge of the plateau runs a rather meagre coral reef which breaks the surface at low tide in some places and helps to protect the shores. The islands of Cuba and the Bahamas give further protection. North of Miami, the coast is exposed to waves coming in from the ocean and, above Cape Canaveral, there is a change to subtropical conditions. Despite the warmth of the sea, the shores are not very rich in animal life because there is no nearby upwelling of water to bring nutrients to the shore.

The shores of the Florida Keys have a characteristic rock platform which may be flat or steeply angled on different beaches. Starting from the

limit of land vegetation, the platform shows four distinct zones of coloration running along the shore. At the top is a white line, a supralittoral zone with sandhoppers, hermit crabs and *Sesarma cinereum*. This crab passes water out of its gill chambers for aeration like the mangrove crab *Aratus pisoni*, but does it more efficiently so that it can stay out of water for a long time. Mangroves grow in this zone, below which is a grey zone still well above the tidemark but with algae growing on exposed roots of trees, and periwinkles and crabs mingling with spiders and earthworms. The looping snail *Truncatella* which pulls and pushes along like a caterpillar, is also found here. The black zone is covered by the spring tides and is coloured by algae. This is the best region for periwinkles and other marine snails, while below it comes the littoral zone with a yellow band containing barnacles, mussels and rock crabs.

North of the Keys, the Florida coastline has long stretches of sandy beaches, as at Marineland and Daytona Beach. Cape Canaveral, until it became associated with the space programme, was a headland of sand dunes and marshes. The exposure to waves means that the sand is shifted along the shore by tidal and wave currents and the outcrops of rock are often inundated with sand. In consequence, there is a rather poor community of animals and plants along these shores, although there may be huge numbers of sand fleas or *Emerita* sand bugs. These are small crabs which burrow in the sand and collect food particles on their feathery antennae as waves wash over them. Sand fleas are often collected for bait by fishermen. Although tropical species dwindle between Miami and Marineland, conditions are still not favourable for the mass of temperate species.

Among the most noticeable species here are barnacles, ghost crabs and *Siphonaria*, the false limpet. The false limpet is unusual because it is descended from land-living ancestors that have returned to the shore, becoming identical in appearance and habits with common limpets. The barnacles include those with the scientific name of *Chthalamus* (pronounced ker-thalamus). Only a minute difference in the shape of the operculum or 'trap door' in the top of the shell reveals the difference between *Chthalamus* and *Balanus* barnacles. Where the two kinds inhabit the same shore, *Chthalamus* is found higher up, reaching the splash zone on wave-exposed shores. Where surf breaks high, *Chthalamus* opens up and furiously collects food from the water as it drains off the rocks. *Balanus* cannot survive the intermittent wetting in which *Chthalamus* thrives. An Italian scientist

Right : Chthalamus barnacles are little different from Balanus barnacles but they live farther up the shore
Far right, top : The false limpet is a curiosity because it is descended from land-dwelling ancestors unrelated to the common limpet
Far right, bottom : Ghost crabs are so named because they seem to vanish when they merge with the sand

Left : The coast near Naples, Florida, where the sea is pushing sand ashore and forming huge dunes

researching into the effects of such exposure has found that *Chthalamus* survives with only two days wetting in every three months and has even lived for two months under a coating of vaseline. Like several other animals living high up the shore, prolonged immersion in water is more damaging to it than prolonged drought.

The *Ocypode*, ghost crabs, also known as racing crabs or sand crabs, are common on tropical sands and spread up American shores to the Carolinas. They get their name from their apparent ability to disappear in a trice. The sand may be covered with thousands of these small crabs, yet they are barely visible as they scuttle away because their colouring is almost the same as that of the sand. Only their shadows make a visual contrast so when the crabs stop and lower their bodies to the sand, the shadows disappear and so do the crabs. Ghost crabs live in burrows as deep as 120 centimetres (4 feet). Some species remove sand from the burrow, spread it over the surface and trample it flat, apparently as a camouflage, but others leave the sand in balls and may cover the burrow entrance with a dome of sand. At low tide the crabs emerge to feed. They pick clean any animal remains, and sometimes capture small fishes at the tide's edge or baby turtles making their way to the sea.

West Indian Shores

Tucked between the angle of South and Central America and hemmed in by the Antillean chain of islands lies the Caribbean Sea. It falls within the Tropic of Cancer and was once the object of European exploration and of great rivalry for the prizes of gold, cane sugar and other exotic crops. Nowadays the Caribbean islands are one of the world's playgrounds. The West Indies are at the southern end of the Antilles, bathed by the South Equatorial Current sweeping in from the equatorial Atlantic. The warmth and clarity of the water are excellent for bathing and skin diving, but the lack of nutrient materials does not make the most ideal environment for a teeming shore community.

Part of the attraction of holidaying in the West Indies lies in its long stretches of sandy beach. By the processes of erosion and longshore drift, headlands have been worn away and material from them has accumulated in sheltered stretches. The headlands are not so full of animal life as we might hope because they are exposed to heavy wave action. Sally Lightfoot crabs scramble over the rocks and some interesting things turn up in rock pools. Among them are octopuses, a food keenly sought by local people who call them sea cats. The proper home of octopuses is in the

Left: The clear waters
of the Caribbean are an
attraction for skindivers
but this means there is
little food for marine
life
Below: Land crabs live
in forests behind the
beach but they must go
down to the sea to
breed

sublittoral zone but like so many of the animals here, they occasionally stray up the shore. Octopuses like to hide in caves and crevices, waiting to seize incautious animals in their arms. Their size is often exaggerated, but the parrot beak lying at the centre of the ring of arms can certainly deliver a poisonous and extremely painful bite.

Sandy beaches are the home of the ubiquitous ghost crabs, and they are replaced in the forests behind the beach by land crabs. These land crabs are formidable creatures; the large West Indian species *Cardisoma* can measure 60 centimetres (2 feet) across its outstretched legs. All species are well adapted to the land and return to the sea only to breed. They live in deep burrows and will climb trees to gather palm fruits. In Florida they are even a pest of tomato farms.

The top of the sandy beach is the haunt of the sea cockroaches, also known as sea slaters or boat roaches (*Lygia*). These creatures, which look like big woodlice and are related to them, feed on pieces of cast-up seaweed. At the bottom of the beaches there are wedge shells which are known as hammer shells. This is because of the way that the shell appears to be hammered into the sand as the mollusc buries itself after being exposed by a wave. Also in the sublittoral fringe are conch shells, small specimens of which come in from the sublittoral zone proper. Conches are prized as food and their heavy shells make good ornaments. The shells have been used as trumpets by Aztecs, Japanese, and both the Ancient and Modern Greeks. Conches feed on seaweeds and push their heavy shells along with thrusts of the foot, using the sharp operculum as a bizarre form of barge pole.

The beaches of the Caribbean are now invaded by house mice, imported accidentally from Europe, which come down in search of seeds washed up by the waves and anything else edible. They are joined by iguana lizards and by mongooses which were imported from India to control snakes, but have become a pest themselves. Birds, including many waders and the reef heron, also comb the beaches in search of food.

Beyond the beaches, and perhaps only 50–100 metres (55–110 yards) offshore, there may be a fringe of coral reef. Here we may find a variety of prettily coloured shrimps and hear the loud clicks which give away the presence of a pistol shrimp (*Alpheus*). Pistol shrimps have one pincer enlarged to form a mechanism like the hammer of a revolver. One arm of the pincer is drawn back and locked. When released it snaps shut sharply and creates a shock wave sufficient to stun nearby

fishes. One captive pistol shrimp even shattered the glass jar in which it was kept.

While on the reef, the casual wader must take precautions against cuts, as well as great care not to tread on any of the large sea-urchins that lie among the coral. Some of them have long spines which are needle-sharp and carry hooks along their length. These drive into the flesh and snap off. The spines of some urchins are coated with a mild poison which makes their presence quite painful. However, the effects soon wear off and the spine is eventually dissolved by our body fluids. Only in the worst cases is medical treatment needed. These sea-urchins are the bane of reef explorers throughout the tropics and, like the universal mangroves, conches and ghost crabs, which are found on the fringes of warmer waters, serve to reinforce rather painfully how cosmopolitan many seashore organisms are.

Another cosmopolitan group of animals are the sea turtles, which feed and breed in shallow tropical seas. Once abundant in the West Indies, turtles have been devastated by the demands for their shells, their eggs and for their calipee – the gelatinous cartilage that is used in turtle soup. Most turtles feed on small marine animals, including jellyfish, but the green turtle (*Chelonia mydas*) is vegetarian and grazes on eelgrass and turtle grass growing in shallow water. Every year, female turtles come ashore at night to lay their eggs in the sand above the high-tide mark. They dig a hole with their hind-flippers, lay a clutch of eggs and return to the sea before daybreak. Eventually the baby turtles hatch out, again at night, and struggle clear of the sand to rush in a mass seawards in an attempt to evade ghost crabs, snakes, dogs and the other predators that haunt the shore.

The Antarctic Coast

The waters of the Southern Ocean encircling the Antarctic continent are extremely rich, supporting huge quantities of planktonic animals. These feed uncounted penguins and other seabirds, as well as seals, fishes, squid and, before their numbers were severely reduced by hunting, the great whales. The richness extends to the life of the sublittoral zones where seaweeds, fishes and many invertebrate animals abound. However, the shore presents a complete contrast, with the rocks and beaches almost devoid of life. This is not surprising; the air temperature drops well below freezing and, perhaps more important, the shore freezes over for much of the year. When the sea temperature drops below its freezing point of $-1.9\,°C$ ($28.6\,°F$), the ebbing tide leaves a thin film of ice that covers everything. The ice accumulates with the addition of snow and is stranded at low tide, effectively preventing colonization by plants and animals. However, during the short Antarctic summer, there is some life on rocky shores.

Not far above the low-tide mark there is a band of the red alga, *Porphyra*, a close relative of the purple laver of North Atlantic. If there is no *Porphyra*, there may be some filamentous green algae. Rockpools are sometimes encrusted with red coralline and on this part of the shore there are

stranded fishes, amphipods and an occasional specimen of krill, the shrimp-like crustacean that forms the bulk of the great whales' diet. True littoral animals are limited to the Antarctic limpet (*Patinigra antarctica*) a bivalve mollusc with a mussel-like habit, and a few amphipod crustaceans and worms hiding under stones. The limpet spreads up from the sublittoral zone to feed on the scant algae. Both algae and limpets are restricted to the sides of boulders where they avoid scraping by ice floes. The limpets cannot survive prolonged freezing and before the shore ices up, they migrate to deeper water.

The antarctic shore is the hunting ground of two birds, the southern black-backed gull (*Larus dominicanus*) and the sheathbill (*Chionis alba*). This gull, like many others, is a fish eater turned scavenger and the shore is only one of its sources of food. It seeks anything edible among the weeds and pools and knocks a considerable number of limpets from their anchorages. The sheathbill is a white, pigeon-like bird, distantly related to the waders. Although it has the distinction of being the only antarctic landbird because it does not have webbed feet, it can swim quite well. Sheathbills forage along the shore like the gull but get most of their summer food scavenging from penguin rookeries.

Above : The sea ice breaks up in the Antarctic summer but shore life cannot get underway until the anchored ice melts
Above right : The elephant seal, largest of the seals, breeds on beaches around Antarctic islands
Right : The sheathbill is a strange pigeon-like bird that scavenges on Antarctic beaches and in penguin colonies

Previous pages : Unlike seabirds which nest above the shore, the emperor penguins lay their eggs just offshore on floating ice

Bibliography

BARRETT, J. *Life on the Seashore* (Collins, London 1958)

BARRETT, J. and YONGE, C. M. *Pocket Guide to the Seashore* (Collins, London 1973)

BURTON, M. *The Margins of the Sea* (F. Muller, London 1954)

CARSON, R. *The Edge of the Sea* (Panther, London 1973; New American Library, New York 1971)

DAKIN, W. J. *The Australian Seashore: a guide for the beach lover, the naturalist, the shore fisherman and the student* (Angus & Robertson, Sydney 1952)

DARWIN, Charles *Geological Observations on Coral Reefs, Volcanic Islands and on South America* (Smith & Elder, London 1851; R. West, New York 1896)

GREEN, J. *The Biology of Estuarine Animals* (Sidgwick & Jackson, London 1968; University of Washington 1968)

INGLE, R. *A Guide to the Seashore* (Hamlyn, London 1969)

LEWIS, J. R. *The Ecology of Rocky Shores* (Biology Science Texts, English Universities Press, London 1964)

MACGINTIE, G. E. and MACGINTIE N. *Natural History of Marine Animals* (McGraw-Hill, New York 1968)

NEWELL, R. C. *The Biology of Intertidal Animals* (Elek Science, London 1970; American Elsevier, New York 1970)

PILKINGTON, R. *The Ways of the Sea* (Routledge & Kegan Paul, London 1968)

RICKETTS, E. and CALVIN, J. *Between Pacific Tides* (Stanford University Press, California 1968)

SOUTHWARD, A. J. *Life on the Seashore* (Heinemann Educational, London 1965; Harvard University Press, Cambridge, Mass. 1965)

STEERS, J. A. *The Sea Coast* (New Naturalist, Collins, London 1953)

STEPHENSON, T. and STEPHENSON, A. *Life Between Tidemarks on Rocky Shores* (W. H. Freeman, London 1972)

THORSON, G. *Life in the Sea* (Weidenfeld & Nicolson, London 1971; McGraw-Hill, New York 1971)

YONGE, C. M. *The Biology of Coral Reefs* in *Advances in Marine Biology* F. S. Russell (Ed) (Academic Press, London and New York 1973)

YONGE, C. M. *The Seashore* (Fontana, London 1969; Atheneum, New York 1964)

The photographs in this book are reproduced by permission of the following:
Pages 2–3 N. Cirani; 4–5 Jacana/Stoll; 6–7 P2; 8 Beaujard-Cedri-Poggio; 9 Photair/A. Perceval; 10 (top) G. Mazza; 10 (bottom) Heather Angel; 11 IGDA; 12 G. Costa; 14 (top) P. Popper; 14 (bottom) E. Dulevant; 15 Z.F.A.-Pictor; 17 P2; 18 N. Cirani; 20 N. Cirani; 21 P2; 22–3 N. Cirani; 24 Folco Quilici; 25 G. Gualco; 27 L. Pellegrini; 28 L. Pellegrini; 29 Jacana; 31 Jacana; 33 Explorer/A. Weiss; 34–5 Jacana/ G. Trouillet; 35 Jacana/A. Kerneis; 36 Jacana/H. Chaumeton; 37 Heather Angel; 38 Jacana/F. Winner; 39 Jacana/A. Ducrot; 40 Jacana/ H. Chaumeton; 41 Jacana/H. Chaumeton; 42 (top) Jacana/K. Ross; 42 (bottom) Heather Angel; 42–3 Heather Angel; 43 (top) Jacana/ F. Winner; 43 (bottom) Heather Angel; 44 D. Pellegrini; 46 (left) Heather Angel; 46–7 Heather Angel; 47 (left) Jacana/F. Winner; 47 (right) Heather Angel; 48 (left) G. Mazza; 48–9 Jacana/J. Dubois; 49 Jacana/F. Winner; 50 (left) Heather Angel; 50 (right) Heather Angel; 51 (top) G. Mazza; 51 (bottom) Heather Angel; 52 Jacana/Brossit; 53 (top) Jacana/H. Chaumeton; 53 (bottom) G. Gualco; 54 L. Pellegrini; 55 Jacana/Vasserot; 56–7 Heather Angel; 58–9 D. Pellegrini; 59 (top) Jacana/F. Winner; 59 (bottom) Jacana/A. Kerneis; 60 Heather Angel; 61 G. Mazza; 62 L. Pellegrini; 63 Jacana/K. Ross; 64 Heather Angel; 65 Jacana/H. Chaumeton; 66 (top) Jacana/F. Winner; 66 (bottom) Jacana/S. Yoff; 67 (top) Heather Angel; 67 (bottom) Jacana/S. Yoff; 68 Jacana/F. Winner; 69 Jacana/K. Ross; 70 Jacana/H. Chaumeton; 71 (top) Jacana/F. Winner; 71 (bottom) Jacana/J. Sardou; 72–3 Heather Angel; 74–5 D. Pellegrini; 75 (top) Jacana/H. Chaumeton; 75 (bottom) Heather Angel; 76 P2; 77 Jacana/S. Yoff; 78 Jacana/S. Yoff; 79 Jacana/ J-M. Bassot; 80 L. Pellegrini; 82 G. Annunziata; 83 L. Pellegrini; 84 L. Pellegrini; 85 (top) Heather Angel; 85 (bottom) Heather Angel; 86–7 Jacana/Rebouleau; 88–9 Jacana/Arthus-Bertrand; 90 (top) Jacana/ F. Henrion; 90 (bottom) Jacana/F. Henrion; 91 Jacana/F. Henrion; 92–3 L. Pellegrini; 94 Heather Angel; 95 (top) Heather Angel; 95 (bottom) Jacana/A. Kerneis; 96 N. Cirani; 98 Time-Life; 99 Explorer/ E. Saint-Servan; 100 (top) Jacana; 100 (bottom) Jacana/Frederic; 101 (top) G. Valet; 101 (bottom) Jacana/W. MacWaren; 102 Danish Travel Association/I. Aistrup; 103 M. Pedone; 104–5 IGDA; 106 (bottom) Jacana/C. Carre; 106–7 L. Pellegrini; 107 (bottom) Jacana/S. Yoff; 108 N. Cirani; 109 (top) Carl E. Östman Ab; 109 (bottom) Nancy Palmer-J. Alexander; 110–11 N. Cirani; 112 T. Poggio; 113 Jacana/ G. Annunziata; 114 (top) G. Gualco; 114 (bottom) G. Mazza; 114–15 P2; 116 N. Cirani; 117 (left) Jacana/H. Chaumeton; 117 (right) Jacana/ S. Yoff; 118 Beken of Cowes; 119 Jacana/S. Yoff; 120 (top) Jacana/ J. Dubois; 120 (bottom left) Foto Bolla; 120 (bottom right) Jacana/ G. Annunziata; 121 Jacana/H. Chaumeton; 122–3 AFA; 124 Explorer/ J. Prevost; 125 (top) Jacana/G. Bonhomme; 125 (bottom) Jacana/ J-Y. Boisson; Endpapers Heather Angel.

Index